THE ROYAL YACHT
Britannia

THE ROYAL YACHT
Britannia

ANDREW MORTON

ORBIS · LONDON

Printed in Spain by Grijelmo, S.A.
ISBN 0-85613-715-4

CONTENTS

PROLOGUE

'The royal yacht Britannia gives the arrival of the Queen a magical majesty that nothing on earth can rival.'

Scene: Palm trees sway gently in the warm morning breeze. Grass-skirted maidens stand in groups on the bleached white beach, chatting gaily. Nearby, smartly uniformed officials anxiously scan the far horizon, waiting nervously.

First she is simply a speck on the horizon, then her sleek shape is silhouetted against the dreamy blue sky. The royal yacht *Britannia* has arrived, bringing the Queen and Prince Philip to the tiny island of Tuvalu in the South Seas. It is a poor man's paradise, the merest blush of pink on the globe, a land where the Queen is affectionately called 'Misis Kwin' and where warmth and informality reign supreme.

The royal couple transfer from the gleaming royal barge to two colourful native canoes, built in one weekend for £150 each and decked out with flowers plucked from the shore. As twenty-six brawny natives hoist the Queen and canoe to their shoulders, the waiting crowds sing and chant their welcome. Misis Kwin has arrived.

Offshore, like some benign royal Jeeves, *Britannia* lies waiting patiently for her mistress to return.

Scene: Four months later on a dull cold day in San Diego, California, in February 1983. One of the richest cities in the wealthiest nation on earth. Thousands of miles and a civilization apart from that South Sea shore. But the welcome is just as warm. A twenty-one-gun salute booms out. *Britannia* cleaves through the choppy iron-grey water, leaving a flotilla of small craft fluttering and cheering behind her, like so many anxious courtiers attending her regal progress.

The yacht, her dark blue hull immaculate, looks the epitome of Edwardian elegance. An empress of the Old World allowing the New World to pay homage. For it is *Britannia* that has given the arrival of the Queen a drama and excitement, a magical majesty, that nothing else can rival.

When the world is your stage it helps to be able to make a dramatic entrance. As a loyal servant to the central players in the continuing royal saga, *Britannia* regularly gives an Oscar-winning performance. Even that old seafarer, Lord Mountbatten, was impressed by her presence. He once wrote, 'I well remember the great thrill of being taken on board the royal yacht, *Victoria and Albert*, and still feel the same sense of excitement whenever I have the honour to embark on the royal yacht *Britannia*.'

She has travelled more than 720,000 miles, visited over 580 ports and circumnavigated the world seven times. Over the years the royal family has come to love and cherish her. She is as much a part of the family as Balmoral and Sandringham, and on board her the royal family have learnt to paint and photograph, have played the fool on deck and sung sea shanties around the black baby grand piano.

Britannia holds a special place in the Queen's heart, and in Prince Philip's words, 'She is special for a number of reasons. Almost every previous sovereign has been responsible for building a church, a castle, a palace or just a house. William the Conqueror built the Tower of London, Edward I built the Welsh castles, Edward IV built St George's Chapel at Windsor . . . and Edward VII built Sandringham. The only comparable structure built in the present reign is *Britannia*. As such she is a splendid example of contemporary British design and technology and much admired wherever she is seen, particularly on official visits overseas.'

Britannia is a complex mixture of contradictions. She is called a yacht, yet she carries a crew of 276 and can even find space for a gleaming Rolls Royce if required. A palace of the waves, yet designed on the lines of the humble North Sea ferry. She communicates to the world using a sophisticated satellite system, yet her crew pad around in rubber-soled shoes and talk by hand signals. Although she is one of the most famous ships in the Royal Navy, she is the least known.

When the royal family are on board nothing is too much trouble. She has even taken a detour to post an important letter, and on Royal birthdays, greetings cards have been delivered by helicopter. All part of the service. She carries a twenty-six piece Royal Marine band which plays at eight in the morning for the ceremony of hoisting colours or late into the night during dinners. In this floating palace it can take three hours to set the table for dinner, and yet the Princess of Wales can wander around barefoot, a bowl of cornflakes in her hand.

As an old trouper, *Britannia* has criss-crossed the globe many times in her years of service. For more than thirty years she has been a willing and trusted servant, dominating the background of the royal stage. Now the First Lady of the Sea sweeps forward to take the spotlight . . . and what an extraordinary tale she has to tell.

Previous page: Palms and flags flutter as the royal yacht Britannia *brings the Queen and Prince Philip to the tropical paradise of Tuvalu during their tour of the South Seas in 1983.*

Left, above and below right: Ruling the waves. The Queen adopts the pose that has become a hallmark of her reign (above); and (below right) carried aloft on a puka – a light hardwood canoe – she makes a dramatic entrance to Tuvalu in the South Pacific. It was the first time the islanders had had the chance of welcoming their sovereign, an event made possible by the royal yacht.

Far left: With the Prince and Princess of Wales on board for their honeymoon, Britannia *arrives at Port Said, Egypt, for their meeting with the Sadats.*

1

PAST AND PRESENT

Yacht – 'A vessel of State usually employed to convey princes, ambassadors or other great personages from one kingdom to another.'

FALCONER'S MARINE DICTIONARY, 1771

When ship number 691 slipped slowly and gracefully down the greased ways into the river Clyde at John Brown's shipyard, in April 1953, she was joining a long and illustrious line.

The royal yacht, named *Britannia* by the Queen and christened not on a tide of champagne but with a bottle of Empire wine crashed against her bow, had a colourful history to live up to.

Kings and queens of England have always relied heavily on their navies, but it wasn't until the seventeenth century and King Charles II that the first royal yacht was recorded in the history books. For a £100 wager the King challenged his brother, the Duke of York, to produce a vessel that could beat his own favourite in a race from Greenwich to Gravesend and back. The result was a draw, but the date, 1661, marks the start of royal yachting in England.

The word yacht is derived from the Dutch *jaghte* and *jagen*, meaning to hunt or chase. Charles took this literally when he fled from Roundhead pursuers after a Royalist defeat at Worcester. He boarded a fast boat at Brighton, sailing for France and safety. The romantic royal became so attached to the boat that he changed her name from *Surprise* to *Royal Escape*, and proudly opened her for public view on the Thames when he was restored to the throne.

During his exile in Holland he was introduced to yachts, immediately falling in love with the sport of racing. His passion for sailing was boundless, and he had a number of yachts in quick succession. But it was the 50-ft (15.2-m) *Mary*, named after his sister, which is credited as being the first ever royal yacht. His undoubted favourite, however, was a sumptuous craft called *Fubbs* – meaning plump or chubby – so named after his pet name for his mistress, the Duchess of Portsmouth.

On board, Charles combined high living with lavish decoration. His royal bedroom was a masterpiece of carved oak panelling, with a huge four-poster bed resplendent with gold brocade and silk. Everything was done to ensure that the royal yacht looked the part of First Lady of the Fleet. This attention to appearance has persisted right down to the current yacht: as Falconer remarks in his *Marine Dictionary*, 'Royal yachts are generally elegantly furnished and richly ornamented with sculpture.'

Charles was certainly a good sailor and clearly enjoyed seeing the discomfiture of those aristocratic landlubbers who came on board simply for an afternoon of revelry. During one rough voyage on the Thames, the Comte de Comines records: 'The king was amused to see all the others sick in the stern and cared little about exposing us to it.'

One of Charles II's last cruises in 1680 nearly ended in tragedy when he and the Duke of York ended up 'handling the sails like common seamen' in order to save the yacht from the sea. On board was the Rev. John Gostling. As they sailed down the Thames the King joined him in song, but the pleasure jaunt quickly turned to a struggle for survival in gale-force winds before eventually, weary and soaked, they limped into Ramsgate. Gostling was so relieved to be saved from a watery end that he wrote the words of the anthem 'They that go down to the sea in ships' which he persuaded his friend, the composer Henry Purcell, to set to music.

Between 1660 and 1685 – the date of King Charles II's death – twenty-six royal yachts were built, but for the next century the royal family took little interest in yachting, and the sport lay in the doldrums. The royal yachts that were built were larger cruising ships rather than racers.

The *Royal George*

However, in the Hanoverian period two outstanding royal yachts were constructed – the *Royal Sovereign* in 1804, which was used by George III for cruises to his favourite resort of Weymouth, and the *Royal George*.

In those days security was neither as strict nor was the monarch as popular as at present. On one occasion, when the *Royal Sovereign* was being refitted at Deptford, some well-dressed visitors came alongside in a rowing boat and asked to look around. The Captain, John Boteler, took the arm of the prettiest lady and was showing the group around when they heard the cry of 'man overboard'.

What had happened was that one of the male visitors had abused the King's name in front of the yacht's master, a fiery Welshman called Franklin. The master was showing off a richly decorated staircase at the entrance to the royal apartments when the uninvited interloper remarked 'Ah, just the thing for fat George when beastly drunk to roll down.' Franklin was so annoyed that he picked the fellow up and kicked him overboard, and the rest of the party would

Previous page: Queen Victoria's favourite yacht, the Victoria and Albert II, *leaves Boulogne after a visit in 1860. This powerful paddle steamer – it could sail at 15 knots – served the Queen for more than forty years.*

Above: Guests of Queen Victoria assemble in her cabin to take their leave. This picture (by F. Winterhalter) shows the Queen's move away from Georgian splendour in decoration. Not for her the gilts and brocades of earlier reigns: she preferred simpler, more homely fittings. State rooms were well ventilated and well lighted, giving a sense of space that belied the 40-foot (12-metre) width of the yacht.

have followed suit had it not been for the intervention of Captain Boteler.

In spite of George III's unpopularity, the *Royal George* really caught the public imagination. Built in 1817, she was a magnificent creation, and a contemporary description waxed lyrical: 'The vessel is the most elegant ever seen. The cabin doors are of mahogany, with gilt mouldings and the windows of plate glass. Ornamental devices in abundance are placed in various parts, all highly gilt, and producing a superb appearance.' When she was broken up in 1905 she was the oldest royal yacht in the world and the third oldest in the Royal Navy. In 1902, when she was moved from her moorings to finish her days as an accommodation hulk, the *Daily Graphic* gave her a double-page obituary that would have done justice to a sovereign.

Nelson's old captain, Sir Edward Berry, was her first commander, and on her maiden cruise huge crowds assembled off Brighton to watch her. The Prince Regent went on board, but the house-warming party was such a drunken affair that the ship had to return to Brighton because the passengers could not stomach the rough sea.

In 1822 the *Royal George* carried King George IV to Scotland, although her entrance to Leith was rather undignified – she was towed in by steamer. Among the welcoming party was the famous novelist Sir Walter Scott.

Leith was again the setting for Queen Victoria's first voyage in the *Royal George*, but the journey, in 1842, proved to be her first and last on board – she watched unamused as the yacht was overtaken by coal steamers. Her diary for 30 August 1842 reveals this displeasure: 'We heard, to our great distress, that we had only gone 58 miles since eight o'clock last night. How annoying and provoking this is. We remained on deck all day lying on sofas: the sea was very rough towards evening and I was very ill.' She hired a paddle steamer for the return journey and made certain that the Prime Minister, Sir Robert Peel, knew of her views. Three months later the keel of the paddle steamer, the *Victoria and Albert*, was laid down. No more did royalty go by sail.

Queen Victoria's royal yachts

For the next ten years until she was succeeded by her successor of the same name, the *Victoria and Albert* took the Queen and her husband Prince Albert on twenty voyages, reaching parts of the kingdom that would otherwise have

been virtually inaccessible. During her first voyage she stopped off Falmouth, and the local mayor was so excited at seeing his young Queen that he fell overboard – resplendent in his velvet robes of office and carrying his symbol of authority, a heavy mace.

On that maiden voyage the Queen became the favourite of the crew after an incident involving their entitlement to 'grog', their usual refreshment. The Queen and several titled friends were sitting out of the wind by the paddle box when they noticed the crew standing in groups whispering. Fearing a mutiny she asked an officer what was the matter, and was told that they couldn't get to their grog store because she was sitting by it. When she heard this the Queen said that she would leave the shelter provided she could have a drink as well. A glass was brought to her and she sipped it and said, 'I'm afraid I can only make the same remark I did once before, that I think it would be very good if it were stronger.' The crew were delighted.

In 1855 the second *Victoria and Albert* was launched, a much-needed replacement as the old model had become too small and slow. She was the Queen's favourite, and during her forty-nine years of service carried the royal family more than 150 times, two thirds of those journeys being overseas.

While she was being built debate in the Admiralty raged over whether they should install the tried and tested paddle propulsion or a new-fangled screw propellor. In the end paddles won the day – because of consideration for Queen Victoria. According to one authority she liked 'the measured strokes of the paddle wheels'. Another expert, Commander Crispin, tested both methods and reported, 'I am convinced till further improvement shall have much lessened or entirely removed the shock and vibration arising from the screw itself – a screw ship, as a yacht, will prove a total failure in that vital and important point – the personal comfort of her majesty.' The comfort of the Queen was still uppermost in the minds of the Admiralty a hundred years later when the present *Britannia* was being designed.

Above all, the *Victoria and Albert II* was a homely ship. She had a number of odd features, not least a gimbal table designed by Prince Albert which, because of a brass weight underneath, remained steady whatever the weather. It is now installed in the drawing room of *Britannia*. The upper deck was not scrubbed teak, but covered with a new patent material – linoleum. When Victoria was aboard a carpet was laid.

The style of furnishings moved away from the elegant traditional wood carving and gilded and damask panelling of the old *Royal George* to interiors which resembled those of country mansions. This was the case also in Queen Victoria's other royal yachts – six steam yachts were built during her reign – which reflect a simplicity of taste that bore witness to her dislike of the regal splendour of previous monarchs.

But even on such a homely vessel, albeit 360-ft (110·m) long and weighing 2470 tons, royalty was not immune from the elements. During one excursion to Madeira with the Empress of Austria on board, the yacht came close to sinking. In a letter, one of the Empress's attendants records: 'Each moment a wave dashed like a cannon ball in my place and then went quickly over the deck: in the intervals was heard the shrill sound of the boatswain's whistle, the increasing signals of the commander, the running and cries of the sailors and a frightful crash, which, now I thought, is the moment when we shall all be buried in the deep sea.

'Everything about the Empress was scattered about, looking glass, china broken, her watch thrown from her bed, chairs, tables, nothing escaped in Her Majesty's cabin nor in ours.

'The kitchen all was ruin, the whole service of the Queen, glasses, pitchers, all was clatter and confusion, the terror of the people arose to the highest

Left: Queen Victoria's dining room (above) could comfortably seat eighteen guests. The only decorations were two silver speaking trumpets, mementos of earlier sailing yachts. Prince Albert was largely responsible for the stylistic simplicity of the state rooms. He designed his study and the cosy sitting room. For Queen Victoria's bedroom (below), Prince Albert chose the rosebud pattern chintz fabric. The carpets were red and black Brussels, and the woodwork throughout the state rooms was polished bird's-eye maple.

pitch, for the sailors fell from the masts, broken legs were the consequence.'

Although the yacht was safely delivered, the royal yachts had many more such hair-raising adventures.

After Prince Albert's death in 1861, Queen Victoria confined herself to British coastal waters, letting other royals take the royal yachts abroad. During one journey, a Mediterranean cruise in 1877, on the second yacht named *Osborne* – the first had been the renamed *Victoria and Albert I* – the Prince and Princess of Wales were enjoying the sun when the captain reported that a sea monster had been spotted. It fitted the description of a sighting of a fabulous sea serpent seen off the coast of Sicily late one June afternoon.

Captain Pearson 'distinctly saw the seal-shaped head of immense size, large flappers and part of a huge body', while Lieutenant Haynes 'saw a head, two flappers and about thirty feet of an animal's shoulders. The head was about six feet thick, the neck narrower, about four or five feet; the shoulders about fifteen feet across, the flappers about fifteen feet in length.' Lieutenant Forsyth described it as 'a huge monster, having a head about fifteen to twenty feet in length; the head was round, and full at the crown. The animal was swimming in a south-easterly direction, propelling itself by means of two large flappers or fins.' He also saw a portion of the body of the animal, 'and that part certainly not under forty-five to fifty feet in length'.

The apparition was seen by the three men about 400 yards away looking goggle-eyed through a telescope. It is not recorded what the Prince of Wales' reaction was, although it is certain that he was told and that it became the talk of the royal family.

During the latter part of her reign, Victoria's usual routine was to spend Christmas, January, May, July and August at Osborne House on the Isle of Wight. Royal yachts were in constant use for conveying ministers and other

Above: Taking the air. A heavily muffled Queen Victoria, by now wheelchair-bound, looks out over the Solent from the deck of her beloved yacht, the Alberta. A loyal Indian 'Moonshee' servant was in constant attendance. It was on the Alberta that the Queen's remains were carried from Osborne to her last resting place at Frogmore, Windsor.

Above right: Edward VII shows off his new yacht, the Victoria and Albert III, *to a suitably impressed Nicholas II, the ill-fated Czar of Russia. The fact that the new yacht could sail at 20 knots – a full two knots faster than the Imperial yacht, the* Standart *– would not have been lost on these royal rivals.*

Above: Czarevitch Alexis, who stands with his sailor servant on board Standart. *The Czar and his family were frequent guests of the King during Cowes week.*

officials to her home on the island. Several additional yachts were built to accommodate dignitaries on what became known as 'milk runs'. The *Elfin*, *Fairy* and finally *Alberta*, the most elegant of the Victorian yachts, were all extensively employed. Indeed it was the *Alberta* which carried Queen Victoria's body from Osborne to the mainland from where she was taken to her last resting place at Frogmore, Windsor.

In the course of that dramatic crossing of the Solent the new king on board the new *Victoria and Albert* noticed that the Royal Standard was flying at half mast. When he asked the captain why, he replied, 'The Queen is dead'. 'The King of England lives' replied Edward VII, and with that the standard was hoisted to the mast top.

Queen Victoria was on board the *Victoria and Albert* in 1851 when the first race in what later became known as the America's Cup was held. There were fifteen entrants. Several yachts took the wrong course and the Americans' boat bore away from the others, so that by the time she was rounding the Needles she had secured such a lead that the other yachts were forgotten. This gave rise to the following message being given to the Queen by an excited signalman: 'America first, Your Majesty. There is no second,' he reported breathlessly.

The old Queen loved her second *Victoria and Albert* but the Government had other ideas for a replacement. The imperial competition between Russia, Germany and Britain was such that Britain had to be seen to have the biggest and the best, especially at sea. Nowhere was this contest keener than in the building of royal yachts. By the turn of the century both the Kaiser and the Czar of Russia had yachts which far outclassed the *Victoria and Albert* in both size and speed. So by the late 1890s the race was on to build the supreme steam yacht.

At first the old Queen took a great deal of persuasion – albeit gentle – that

Below: Edwardian elegance. The state dining room on the Victoria and Albert III, *designed in true English Adam style. There was room for thirty guests. Edward VII had an enormous appetite, and hated his concentration on his food to be interrupted by intellectual conversation. He preferred to be entertained by an amusing anecdote or some juicy piece of social gossip relayed by a pretty titled lady. During his reign, however, he gained a reputation as a royal diplomat. His frequent travels on board the royal yacht to the courts of Russia, Italy and Germany sealed his position as an active promoter of British foreign policy. During one international crisis he was photographed walking with the Liberal Prime Minister Campbell-Bannerman. He looked the picture of earnest concern, striking his fist to illustrate a serious point. The caption read: 'Is it peace or war?' But it was food, not foreign policy, that was taxing the King. The Prime Minister later admitted: 'The King wanted to have my opinion on whether halibut is better baked or boiled.'*

the yacht she saw as her home needed replacing. In spite of her reservations, however, plans for the new model went ahead, and the vessel, 80-ft (24.4-m) longer than her predecessor, equipped with twin screw propulsion and costing £510,034, was launched at Pembroke in May 1899.

The engines and masts were fitted, and just as she was about to be taken out of the dock she nearly capsized. She listed alarmingly to starboard, and was left stranded like a whale. Frenzied workmen poured barrowful upon barrowful of concrete into her as ballast before she could be righted. That settled the matter for the Queen – she never set foot inside her.

At the subsequent enquiry it emerged that 771 tons of extra weight had been added to the ship, mainly because nobody dared argue when the Queen made suggestions. A lot may be explained also by the fact that the plans for the yacht had been borrowed from those used to build the Czar of Russia's yacht, and nobody quite knew whether they had been drawn in metric or imperial measure!

In the end, after she was commissioned in July 1901, she had an unblemished career and served three kings well. She made more than sixty voyages before being laid up in 1914 for the First World War. A smaller sister yacht, the *Alexandra*, was built in 1907 and was used for Channel crossings.

The *Victoria and Albert III* was from inside to out a magnificent vessel. Fast, quiet, and sumptuously equipped, she vied with and beat the best in Europe. There were four stairways, and the upper deck was covered with painted canvas which, in fine weather, was overlaid with carpet when the royals were on board. The carpet was over 200-ft (60-m) long, and the unruly material was known as 'the serpent' by the crew. Above the royal writing table were two sketches of heroism and tragedy at the South Pole. The drawings, by A. Wilson, which showed Amundsen's flag in the background, depicted Captain Scott's vain attempt to reach the Pole first.

The elegant dining room could seat thirty guests in comfort. There were

three fine Teheran carpets; the curtains were of silk and the satinwood chairs were Hepplewhite. On the walls were pictures of the naval reviews of 1904 and 1907. Two silver-gilt speaking trumpets and a silver trumpet completed the dazzling display. For after-dinner amusement, Queen Alexandra fired off the nine o'clock gun. She would often surprise guests by pressing a switch at the dinner table which fired the two bronze six-pounders electrically.

Edward VII

Edward VII had his own peccadillos on board. He refused to go anywhere without trainloads of luggage and servants. In 1901 he went to stay with his sister at Friedrichdorf, taking thirty-one servants on board the *Victoria and Albert*. There was even an Arab boy whose sole duty was to make the royal coffee. The luggage was equally prodigious. In the King's trunks alone there would be as many as forty suits and uniforms and twenty pairs of boots and shoes, even for a weekend stay. And of course he would go nowhere without his beloved dog Caesar, a scruffy white and brown fox-terrier. Although Caesar was devoted to the king, he would attack anyone else with relish, particularly long-suffering crew members. The Queen's corgis have similar tendencies.

Lord Hardinge, who went with the king on the royal yacht in 1903, recalled, 'Whenever I went into the King's cabin, this dog always went for my trousers and worried them, much to the King's delight. I used not to take the slightest notice and went on talking all the time to the King, which I think amused His Majesty still more.'

Although he would forgive his Caesar everything, people who transgressed the rules of behaviour on board the royal yacht were harshly dealt with. During a visit to Spain in 1907, he was to meet the British ambassador to Madrid, Sir Maurice de Bunsen. The hapless diplomat didn't know what to wear and so chose close-fitting new white breeches and stockings. As he

Above: Immaculate as always, Edward VII strikes a typically jaunty pose during a visit to Czar Nicholas on the Baltic in 1908.

Right: King Edward makes a point to the debonair King Alphonso of Spain as they enjoy a day out on the racing cutter Britannia during Cowes Week.

climbed aboard the furious king shouted, '*Trousers* are always worn on board ship,' and stormed off.

Proper social dress and behaviour were essential on board the *Victoria and Albert*. Before dinner guests were asked to assemble in the drawing room to await the arrival of the King fifteen minutes later. They presented themselves in full evening dress, the women in long dresses with trains and carrying ostrich-feather fans, and the men in white ties with carnations or gardenias in their buttonholes. If the Queen were present the men wore frock coats and knee breeches. The King always arrived on time, and after making a quick survey of the elegant scene to ensure that there were no late arrivals, led the way to the dining room.

He was always served by a footman in scarlet livery who stood attentively behind his chair. The selected servant had to be sharp on his toes, for the King was an enormous eater who hated to interrupt his concentration on his meal with unnecessary chitchat. A mammoth twelve-course meal was not unknown, and often, to the Queen's anxious concern, he would swallow several dozen oysters before moving briskly on to caviare, chicken and every type of game. These rich repasts would be washed down with several glasses of champagne and rounded off with a fat cigar.

He would relish these feasts all the more after a day's sailing on his beloved sailing yacht *Britannia* during Cowes week.

The *Britannia*, a huge J-class yacht, was built for King Edward when Prince of Wales in 1893 and had an unrivalled career in big sail yachting. When he

died, George V in his turn contributed to her success. Both adored the sleek, nimble vessel and nothing pleased them more than to be at the helm during a big race. King George's adoration bewildered Queen Mary, who would only venture on to the yacht on a very calm day. One August she recorded in her diary, 'The *Britannia* has just passed us by, and I saw the King looking very wet and uncomfortable in oilskins. What a way to enjoy oneself.'

Although George V continued the Cowes tradition, he used the *Victoria and Albert* less frequently than his father. While Edward VII loved his travels on the Continent his son was happier by the home fires. During one long illness he was prevailed upon to take a Mediterranean cruise on board the royal yacht to help restore his health. Grumpily he agreed, but his verdict was not favourable. He declared Naples to have a harbour 'full of dead dogs' and Malta to be a 'bloody place'. The *Victoria and Albert*, however, was still used for those marvellous set piece naval occasions. George V reviewed the Fleet on board her in 1935, and two years later the young Princess Elizabeth joined her father George VI on board the yacht for his Coronation Review in 1937.

Trials at sea

Given the conditions that members of the royal family experienced during their travels, it is a good thing that the by now increasingly unseaworthy *Victoria and Albert* stayed in home waters. During a tour to the South Island of New Zealand in 1927 the Duke of York and his party had to make use of a tug to return to his cruise ship, the *Renown*. The passage was so rough that when he

Left: A typical menu on the Victoria and Albert III. *Edward VII refused to allow a meal to be delayed by iced punch or sorbet, and guests who dawdled over a course were given short shrift by the monarch.*

Below left: Crowds line the shore as the royal yacht sails out to Spithead for the Naval Review in 1911.

Below: King George V, resplendent in full Navy uniform, reviews the Fleet.

Right: Princess Elizabeth chats to her father, George VI, before the Naval Review off Spithead in 1937.

Above: 'We three kings . . .' A rare photograph of Edward VII and the future Kings George V and VI.

reached the *Renown* the Duke (later George VI) had to be dragged on board by two seamen. The Duchess watched the scene from the deck. She wrote later, 'I was glad to be on board when I saw my husband being thrown (literally) from the bridge of the tug on to our quarter deck at Bluff. It looked most unpleasant, but he did not seem to mind much.'

During the same tour, as they made their way home across the Indian Ocean after visiting Australia, the royal couple narrowly missed having to take to the lifeboats when a raging fire broke out in the ship's boiler room.

As seamen battled to put out the blaze, other deckhands stood by to flood the ammunition chamber. *Renown* was on her own, three days sailing from her escort ship. With a heavy sea and lifeboats smashed from previous storms the situation looked grim. Plans were made to abandon ship but, with the flames just feet away from the main tanks, the fire-fighters managed to douse the inferno. Throughout it all Princess Elizabeth's parents remained calm, and afterwards the Duke commented to his father, King George V, 'Oil is a very dangerous substance for a fire and it might have been serious.'

Before the *Britannia*

During the 1930s the pattern of using the *Victoria and Albert* for home ceremonial occasions and requisitioning Royal Navy frigates or cruise liners for overseas tours was established. The continued expense of running the yacht combined with the need for a replacement vexed the Cabinet, but in spite of the country being deep in recession with three million unemployed, they decided to go ahead with a replacement. Prime Minister Neville Chamberlain's Cabinet met in July 1938 and agreed to build a new royal yacht which could double as a hospital ship. The approved cost was £900,000.

Cabinet minutes from that meeting record: 'In the course of the discussion the importance was emphasized of avoiding any possibility that the King might be exposed to criticism by building the yacht. The kind of argument that might be used for political discussion was that money was not available for the unemployed but could be . . . found for a royal yacht.'

The King was 'interested' in the new yacht but 'did not want to press it if there was any risk of interrupting progress with rearmament'. Six months later the tide had turned and Britain was about to be engulfed in the whirlwind of another world war. Reluctantly the Cabinet decided to leave the plan to one side. Sadly the *Victoria and Albert* never saw service again. She acted as a depot ship at Portsmouth during the war, but in 1955 this superb example of a pre-war steam yacht was taken to Faslane and broken up.

Below: End of an era. The Victoria and Albert III *is broken up at Faslane in 1955. The most valuable pieces of furniture were transferred to* Britannia. *Other pieces were sent to various naval establishments. The staircase and doors from the royal apartments went to HMS* Excellent *while the anchor, the wardroom stove and the fireplace from the Queen's drawing room can still be seen on display at the Maritime Museum at Greenwich.*

After the war the policy of commissioning cruise liners and Royal Navy warships for royal tours continued. One such tour was to South Africa in the vicious winter of 1947 on board the battleship, *HMS Vanguard*. It was the first time all the royal family had travelled together. But there was one unwilling participant on this long journey away from the worst winter on record to the warm sun south of the Equator. Princess Elizabeth desperately wanted to shiver back home in the company of the man to whom she had secretly become engaged, Lieutenant Philip Mountbatten.

For nearly a year the couple had to mask their feelings as they strove to keep the engagement quiet. This was at the express wish of the Princess's father, George VI, who did not want news of the engagement to take the spotlight away from the purpose of the tour – to thank the South Africans for joining forces with Britain during the war. Duty must triumph over sentiment, he argued. Duty duly did, although sentiment did squeeze its way in. Before she left from Portsmouth on February 1, Philip gave her a record of a song by Rogers and Hammerstein called 'People will Say We're in Love'. Legend has it she played it over and over on the voyage south.

But there were fun and frolics enough to keep her mind off her naval fiancé. Deck quoits, rifle target practice with her parents, larks with the officers and the hilarious Crossing the Line ceremony. One man who joined in with gusto was a certain Group Captain Peter Townsend, a flying ace chosen by the King to accompany the royal party because of his exceptional war record. In such a magnanimous gesture were the seeds of future unhappiness sown for Princess Margaret and her sovereign sister.

During the visit Princess Elizabeth celebrated her twenty-first birthday with a speech to the Commonwealth; appropriately enough the theme was 'duty'. Just five months later the couple were reunited and their engagement formally announced on 10 July 1947. But there was a shadow over their happiness. For during the cruise the King, his health already sapped by his war work, first noticed the cramps in his legs which were to grow steadily worse and force him to undergo major surgery. As his health declined, the need for a new yacht increased, since it was felt that restful cruises under the Mediterranean sun would help his recovery.

Above and right: On board HMS Vanguard during the cruise to South Africa in 1947, Princess Elizabeth dons a sailor's hat (top). Before she left Britain her father, King George VI, gave his blessing to the secret engagement between his eldest daughter and Lieutenant Philip Mountbatten. During the cruise, the ship's cat had kittens (above), and Princess Elizabeth and Princess Margaret joined in the fun and games on deck (right).

The *Britannia* is born

The Admiralty's chief architect, Sir Victor Shepheard, underlined this soon after *Britannia*'s launch by revealing that: 'The project was undertaken as a matter of urgency since it was the hope that a yacht in which His Majesty could undertake sea voyages would greatly improve the chances of his recovery to good health.'

Before the plans were announced in October 1951 the King insisted, as he had before the war, that economy was to be the watchword. He was sensitive to the fact that in postwar, austerity Britain lavish expenditure on a new royal yacht would only excite criticism.

Sir Victor explained: 'The late King and the Queen both stressed this need for economy and made many suggestions with the object of reducing expenditure.' The plan was still for a yacht which could double as a hospital ship in wartime, and the Admiralty decided that as no naval yard had the necessary experience, the order should go to John Brown's shipyard on the Clyde. The yard, which has produced liners such as the *Queen Elizabeth I* (*QE1*), the *Queen Elizabeth II* (*QE2*) and the *Queen Mary*, were told that speed was essential if the King was to be helped back to health. But the gesture was in vain. The King died in February 1952, four months before the keel of the yacht was laid down.

The young Queen and her Consort, Prince Philip, took a very active interest in the yacht's construction in spite of their new responsibilities. Although economy was still the keynote, it is in many respects its triumph, for *Britannia* is a clever combination of economy and elegance, careful craftsmanship and cunning design. The design constraints were used to advantage, giving her a smooth, sleek exterior and a simple but stylish interior. Every last detail has been painstakingly considered. The funnel, for example, has a special gutter to stop raindrops staining the buff paintwork. Even the 41-ft (12.5-m) long royal barge is tailored to the individual heights of the Queen and Prince Philip to ensure that they can see and be seen.

Her three masts – with the Royal Standard flying at the main, the flag of the Lord High Admiral at the fore and the Union Jack at the mizzen-mast – have decorative tops which are used as aerials. It is touches like this which give the yacht its unique outline – elegant, streamlined, uncluttered. As Sir Hugh Casson, who helped design the interiors, remarked: '*Britannia*'s looks seem to have improved with age.' Ironically, the blueprint for the First Lady of the Fleet was based on designs for two humble North Sea ferries, the *Arnhem* and *Amsterdam*.

John Brown's chief architect, Dr John Brown, now 83, says: 'Our brief was to build a robust structure with an ocean-going capacity. It was also to be an advert for British shipbuilding at its best.' And he recalls a certain thirty-two-year-old naval officer, with no experience of shipbuilding, who often visited. 'You had to be on your toes when Prince Philip was on board,' he says. 'He was very keen and peppered us all with questions. There was one incident when he came on board when the winding gear for the Queen's embarkation ladder jammed. He promptly ordered it out. That was typical of him.' Such interest, some reports claim, prompted the following comment from Sir James McNeil, the managing director of John Browns. At the launch he was asked by the BBC correspondent what he thought of the new yacht. He replied tersely, 'I'm not interested in ferry boats.' A comment which some took to imply exasperation at Prince Philip's interference.

But Dr Brown has nothing but praise for the way Prince Philip worked on the project, and remembers that when the Queen again visited the yard in 1955 she was 'very vigorous' in her appreciation of the yacht.

The installation of stabilizers made journeys in rough seas more comfortable

*Above: 'I name this ship . . .' The new
royal yacht* Britannia *glides into the
Clyde.*

Royal Standard

Union Jack

Main Mast

Mizzen-Mast

White Ensign

Rudder

JOHN·S· SMITH

Starboard Propeller

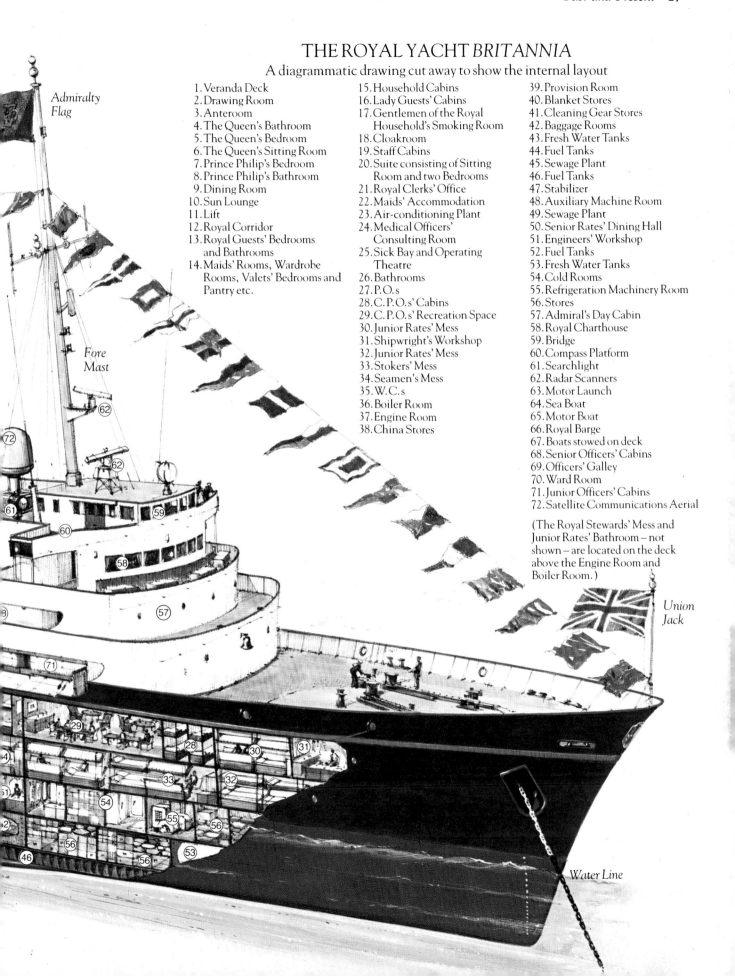

THE ROYAL YACHT *BRITANNIA*

A diagrammatic drawing cut away to show the internal layout

1. Veranda Deck
2. Drawing Room
3. Anteroom
4. The Queen's Bathroom
5. The Queen's Bedroom
6. The Queen's Sitting Room
7. Prince Philip's Bedroom
8. Prince Philip's Bathroom
9. Dining Room
10. Sun Lounge
11. Lift
12. Royal Corridor
13. Royal Guests' Bedrooms and Bathrooms
14. Maids' Rooms, Wardrobe Rooms, Valets' Bedrooms and Pantry etc.
15. Household Cabins
16. Lady Guests' Cabins
17. Gentlemen of the Royal Household's Smoking Room
18. Cloakroom
19. Staff Cabins
20. Suite consisting of Sitting Room and two Bedrooms
21. Royal Clerks' Office
22. Maids' Accommodation
23. Air-conditioning Plant
24. Medical Officers' Consulting Room
25. Sick Bay and Operating Theatre
26. Bathrooms
27. P.O.s
28. C.P.O.s' Cabins
29. C.P.O.s' Recreation Space
30. Junior Rates' Mess
31. Shipwright's Workshop
32. Junior Rates' Mess
33. Stokers' Mess
34. Seamen's Mess
35. W.C.s
36. Boiler Room
37. Engine Room
38. China Stores
39. Provision Room
40. Blanket Stores
41. Cleaning Gear Stores
42. Baggage Rooms
43. Fresh Water Tanks
44. Fuel Tanks
45. Sewage Plant
46. Fuel Tanks
47. Stabilizer
48. Auxiliary Machine Room
49. Sewage Plant
50. Senior Rates' Dining Hall
51. Engineers' Workshop
52. Fuel Tanks
53. Fresh Water Tanks
54. Cold Rooms
55. Refrigeration Machinery Room
56. Stores
57. Admiral's Day Cabin
58. Royal Charthouse
59. Bridge
60. Compass Platform
61. Searchlight
62. Radar Scanners
63. Motor Launch
64. Sea Boat
65. Motor Boat
66. Royal Barge
67. Boats stowed on deck
68. Senior Officers' Cabins
69. Officers' Galley
70. Ward Room
71. Junior Officers' Cabins
72. Satellite Communications Aerial

(The Royal Stewards' Mess and Junior Rates' Bathroom – not shown – are located on the deck above the Engine Room and Boiler Room.)

Admiralty Flag

Fore Mast

Union Jack

Water Line

for the Queen, reputed to be a poor sailor. Extra air-conditioning and laundry facilities and a high cruising speed of 21 knots were all features of the yacht which were incorporated because of its dual role as a hospital ship. But then again not every hospital ship has a 22 by 9ft 6in (6.7 × 2.9m) garage that can accommodate a gleaming Rolls Royce, a strongroom and a wine cellar! It was the Navy's boast that she could be converted into a hospital ship within twenty-four hours. The wards, for 200 patients, are in the royal apartments located in the aft section of the ship. Infectious and TB cases would be installed in the Queen's drawing room, while the operating room, X-ray and pathological laboratory are on the lower deck.

Her shape was modified to give her extra speed as a hospital ship, with a modern clipper bow and cruiser stern instead of the traditional swan bow and counter stern of previous royal yachts. That design feature gave her an extra half knot in trials, but also that unique sleek shape. At 412ft 3in (125.6m) long and 55ft (16.7m) wide, the yacht is half the length of the *QE2*. The secret of her smooth lines lies in the cunning application of naval craftsmanship. Instead of using rivets on the outside of the hull, the builders went back to Victorian techniques and used internal butt straps to give her that smooth, flush finish – yet another feature that distinguishes her from ordinary ships. During her speed trials off the Isle of Arran, the crew, many from the old *Victoria and Albert*, were delighted by their new ship. They were impressed by her speed – she reached 22¾ knots – and the absence of roll. Indeed the only victim of seasickness was Fluff the cat, the ship's mascot. But that was her own fault; she would insist on eating raw meat.

It is surprising therefore that *Britannia* was dubbed 'The Rock and Roll

Above: View from the mizzen-mast. Britannia *refuels at sea.*

Right: Every yacht should have one. The royal Rolls Royce is carefully loaded on board Britannia. *The garage is next to the Queen's wardrobe room, and the limousine can only be squeezed on board by removing the bumpers. During the tricky business of stowing the Rolls the royal barge has to be partially lowered so that the car can be delicately manoeuvred on board. But these days it is rarely carried. 'There's usually a suitable car waiting at the other end', says one yacht officer.*

Above: The Queen arrived at the launch in deep mourning. She told the cheering crowds: 'My father felt most strongly, as I do, that a yacht is a necessity, and not a luxury for the head of our great Commonwealth.' The importance of the event was underlined by the presence of TV cameras – it was one of the first outside broadcasts.

Lady', the 'Awkward Lady' and behaving like 'a top-heavy minesweeper' because she was so unstable. One story suggested that the Queen had to summon help from the crew in the middle of the night because a storm had caused all her furniture to shift, highly improbable in view of the yacht's stabilizers. 'She is an excellent sea-going ship', says one officer.

The speed of the 5,769-ton yacht is due to geared steam turbine engines which can develop a mighty 12,000-shaft horsepower. But it was the boilers providing steam for these engines, which use heavy oil fuel, which caused such controversy during the Falklands war. The Ministry of Defence argued that she could not serve in the South Atlantic as she could not be refuelled – the rest of the fleet ran on diesel. As a result a special tanker would have had to be assigned solely for her use. Impractical given the shortage of tankers. As a result the SS *Uganda* was deemed more suitable. Ironically, one of the many times she has refuelled at sea was near the Falklands during the circumnavigation of the globe by Prince Philip.

But diesel was never considered, because of the noise and vibration of the engines. 'The comfort of Her Majesty was paramount,' says Dr Brown.

Concern with appearance is also an essential aspect of a floating palace. *Britannia*'s hull is dark blue above and red below, with a snowy white superstructure and buff-coloured funnel and masts. There were early problems with that dark blue paint. It simply wouldn't stick, and painters had to strip her down five times before they got the right formula. They were touching her up right until she went on her maiden voyage to meet the Queen and Prince Philip returning from their Commonwealth tour.

As a finishing touch a thin ornamental gold line is painted round her hull. In the overall cost of £2,098,000 for the yacht this gold paint cost just £90 and the labour £150 – but it still had some MPs glossy with rage. Although she is probably the best-known ship in the world, *Britannia* carries no name on her side, merely the royal cypher on her stern and the royal coat of arms painted on her bow.

Indeed, the very name *Britannia* was a closely guarded secret right up to the moment when the Queen said proudly, 'I name this ship *Britannia*,' and sent a bottle of Empire wine crashing against her bows. The name was received with a mixture of surprise and delight by the cheering Clydeside crowd, who broke into a spontaneous chorus of 'Rule Britannia'.

Many had thought she would be named after a member of the royal family, in keeping with tradition: 'Prince Charles' was the bookies' favourite. In court circles some wags suggested updating 'Victoria and Albert' and calling the new yacht, 'Elizabeth and Philip'. The suggestion may have brought a wry smile to the Queen's lips, but she had her own ideas, which stemmed from her personal philosophy of the role of monarchy in modern Britain. She sees this role as being essentially one of representing, and being seen to represent, her subjects. Thus she wanted a name that was familiar, but not family. So *Britannia* it was, a name that also echoed the glory of the old sailing yacht.

The young Queen emphasized the regal and yet public nature of the new yacht at her launch when she said: 'My father felt most strongly, as I do, that a yacht was a necessity, and not a luxury for the head of our great British Commonwealth, between whose countries the sea is no barrier, but the natural and indestructible highway.'

She underlined the view that the new royal yacht was not a personal pleasure craft, but a working palace-at-sea, by allowing the yacht to be opened up to selected visitors after her return from her triumphant Commonwealth tour in 1954. What did these lucky few – mainly pressmen – see of this First Lady of the Fleet during their tour? In fact, what is life like in the world's most famous ship?

2

LIFE ON BOARD
THE FLOATING PALACE

'Working on the royal apartments of Britannia was one of the most interesting experiences of my professional life...'

SIR HUGH CASSON

The royal yacht is a familiar and reassuring friend to the Queen, as comfortable as a favourite armchair where she can relax during a hectic tour. It is easy to see why. For a lady who spends her days in palaces, *Britannia* is home from home. During state visits she is able both to entertain in style and to let her hair down at the end of a long day.

The royal yacht is unique among royal residences in that she combines both the formality of Buckingham Palace and the holiday status of Sandringham and Balmoral. Like any home, *Britannia* contains a mixture of treasured family heirlooms – many from the old *Victoria and Albert* – selected gifts from her travels around the world and knicknacks the Queen has simply taken a fancy to. But unlike most homes, a great many things on board are priceless and irreplaceable. Millions have seen the outside of the Queen's sleek floating

Previous page: The glamour and glitter of a dinner on board Britannia, *on this occasion during the Queen's Silver Wedding anniversary cruise in 1972.*

Below: Detail of the dining room, drawn by Sir Hugh Casson. He was asked to design the yacht's interiors by the Queen after she had rejected the original plans from Britannia's *interior designers, McInnes, Gardner and Partners. Sir Hugh recalls: 'The Queen and Prince Philip felt they were too fussy; elaborate interiors do look ridiculous at sea. Simplicity was the keynote – hence for example the grey carpeting which runs throughout the state apartments. I also wanted to show off the quality of light at sea. The royal couple took a close interest in every aspect of the design. The Queen is a meticulous observer with very strong views; there was no question of showing her a drawing and her saying: "All right, that will do." She had definite views on everything from the door-handles to the shape of the lampshades.'*

palace, but only a few have ever had the privilege of looking around this royal treasure chest. Those who have are deeply impressed by the restrained country house style of its light and airy rooms.

Sir Hugh Casson, an old friend of the royals, was given the daunting task of designing rooms which could function as family, state and hospital quarters, combining the desires of the Admiralty with the wishes of the Queen and Prince Philip.

As Sir Hugh writes in his diary: 'The design of ship interiors has fascinated me . . . and working on the royal apartments of *Britannia* and the public rooms of the P and O flagship *Canberra* were among the most interesting experiences of my professional life.' The Queen was anxious to keep down costs while at the same time incorporating a sense of tradition in the design, hence the large number of fittings saved from the third *Victoria and Albert*.

Prince Philip brought his own brand of robust flamboyance to design problems. He had a novel approach to testing the ability of the new dining room to cope with state banquets on board. The Prince decided that the table was not big enough and so took various Buckingham Palace aides and servants to Portsmouth on the train. They duly trooped on board the royal yacht and were seated on the thirty-two Hepplewhite chairs at the ebony-edged, mahogany dining table while cooks served up a dinner from the all-electric kitchen below. He made his point – the table simply wasn't big enough to cope with large banquet occasions. As a result two wings were added and fourteen extra chairs bought to bring the seating to fifty-six.

As a practical extra, Lord Mountbatten came up with the idea for an ingenious electrified table runner so that specially adapted candelabra could be spiked in anywhere along the table.

Dining Room.

'The few VIPs who have had the privilege of looking round this royal treasure chest are deeply impressed by the restrained country house style of its light and airy rooms.'

The use of furniture from the old *Victoria and Albert* meant that the entire cost for interior decoration was only £78,000 while the carpets added a mere £9000. No wonder that newspaper correspondents were amazed when they first stepped on board *Britannia* just after she returned from her maiden voyage in 1954. 'The big surprise was the lack of luxury,' said the *Daily Mail*, somewhat taken aback. Indeed even the crisp white linen on the Queen's bed was sixty years old – it was taken from Queen Victoria's rooms on the second *Victoria and Albert*. Correspondents noted that the carpets were wearing thin and that some guest rooms – including that used by Prime Minister Winston Churchill – had bare boards.

The royal apartments

That state of affairs has long since been remedied. A huge wall-to-wall silver-grey carpet now runs throughout the state rooms. In the drawing room this is overlaid with three beautiful Persian carpets, one given by the Emir of Abu Dhabi, the other two by the Ruler of Quatar during the Queen's tour there in 1979.

In the royal apartments the colour scheme is restrained, with white-painted walls, brass metalwork and mahogany. Pastel shades and bright chintzy fabrics are the style of the guest bedrooms. When Prime Minister Margaret Thatcher was shown round by Rear Admiral Greening, she very much approved of the Queen's choice, the furnishings and colour scheme matching her own tastes.

It is to Sir Hugh Casson's credit that the Queen's apartments look so spacious and impressive, and even the *Architect's Journal* of 1954 was forced to concede: 'The architect's restraint has retained an atmosphere of space which could have easily been destroyed.'

Below: A Casson sketch of the anteroom and drawing room. Sir Hugh says: 'For these two rooms the overall idea was to give the impression of a country house at sea. I think we succeeded. Even today the yacht looks very striking. She has an attractively old-fashioned air about her.'

Ante-Room & Drawing Room.

Below: The tattered White Ensign flown on Captain Scott's sledge during his ill-fated Antarctic expedition. In 1912, when his body was found, it was removed and a year later presented to George V.

Centre: A Casson sketch of the drawing room. During the design discussions with the Queen and Prince Philip, debate raged as to whether or not to have an open fireplace as a focal point for the room. Sir Hugh even went as far as looking up Merchant Navy law on the subject. He recalls: 'I discovered that Navy practice meant that if you had an open fire you also had to have a sailor standing by with a bucket. This was clearly ridiculous.' (The fire is electric.)

Bottom: The gimbal table, designed by Prince Albert, which stays steady in the worst storms. It is now in the drawing room.

The Queen's apartments are aft, at the rear of the yacht, while all the crew's accommodation is forward. When you walk down the wide mahogany staircase which leads to the yacht's state apartments you have the same feeling as you do when passing through the grand entrance of a palace, which indeed is precisely what *Britannia* is.

In this section of the yacht scarcely a nautical note intrudes. Tall mahogany doors link the anteroom with the drawing room. These can be folded back to give an expansive 55-ft (16.7-m) wide reception room where the Queen can host receptions for up to 250 guests. A mahogany bookcase from the old *Victoria and Albert* dominates the anteroom, while on the wall is a symbol of bravery and endurance – a tiny, tattered White Ensign carefully kept in a glass case. It was flown by Captain Scott on his sledge during his vain but heroic attempt to reach the South Pole. The flag was found by his body when it was recovered in 1912 and given to King George V a year later.

Walking from the anteroom to the drawing room gives you a more nautical,

but homely feeling. This room too contains pieces from the *Victoria and Albert*, including a satinwood desk which belonged to Queen Victoria and that eternally upright gimbal table designed by the ingenious Prince Albert. In the corner is a TV set – a video has recently been added – a baby grand piano, an attractive electric fireplace and, so that you never forget whose room you are in, there is a knighting stool where those who have served the Queen well kneel to receive their honours.

Over the electric fireplace is an oil painting showing *Britannia* returning to the Pool of London after her maiden voyage. On the walls are photographs and paintings of previous royal yacht admirals, including Sir Berkeley Milne who commanded the royal yacht in 1903. Landscape artist Edward Seago, who joined Prince Philip during his circumnavigation of the globe, has several of his strong, bold oils on display.

As you look round these spacious apartments your eyes light on the scores of mementos from the Queen's many foreign tours. There is a strange-looking *ike*

Below: The satinwood desk belonging to Queen Victoria.

Bottom: The elegant mahogany bookcase originally placed in the King's study in the old Victoria and Albert III. *It is now in the anteroom.*

Below: The Queen's sitting room. It is streamlined to essentials, with a seven-foot (2.1-m) long desk, telephone and dictaphone system.

(a mallet used by the women of Tonga) and a *porai* (a fighting club used by their menfolk) which the Queen was given when she visited in 1970. There are many ethnic gifts, some from the South Seas, like the shark carved in driftwood by Pitcairn islanders to commemorate the royal visit in 1971. All adult islanders took the trouble to sign it on the back. Predictably, many presents have a nautical flavour, like the antique sword dating from 1786 which the Swedish Navy gave Her Majesty after a state visit in 1956.

Retrace your steps from the drawing room, back through the anteroom, from which the studies and sitting rooms of the Queen and Prince Philip lead off. In these rooms sentiment is the keynote in the decoration. The Queen's sitting room is streamlined to essentials, with a 7-ft (2.1-m) long built-in desk with a green leather top, complementing the moss-green carpet. A mirror in the style of a ship's wheel and topped with a crown takes pride of place above the electric fire. Memories of her first Commonwealth tour on the SS *Gothic* are retained, with a settee and armchair and light brackets painted in the old silver brought from the ship and installed in her sitting room.

One deck below are the offices of the private secretaries with dictaphones, typewriter and four tiers of filing cabinets. Both the Queen and Prince Philip have telephones which can be 'scrambled' for secret conversations.

Prince Philip's study is far more masculine, with teak panelling, a red-topped desk and a settee and easy chair in oatmeal hopsack. It is carpeted in grey and curtained with navy and white printed linen. When he was told that the curtains were getting frayed he shrugged it off saying, 'If they are swapped round it won't show.' The striking feature of his room is an illuminated glass

HMY Britannia.
Her Majesty's Sitting Room.

Below: Prince Philip's sitting room. An illuminated case with a model of his first command, HMS Magpie, has pride of place in this essentially masculine room.

case containing a scale model of his first and only command, HMS *Magpie.* Before George VI died Prince Philip was on the brink of an illustrious naval career, and when he is on board he takes an active interest in the running of the yacht. In the early days it was not unknown for him to join the 'watches'.

His room furnishings are not entirely naval. During a visit to New Zealand he spotted a reproduction of a painting of the Queen by Edward Halliday. He asked the hotel manager if he could have it, and it now adorns his cabin.

From her sitting room, the Queen takes a short ride in a lift to her bedroom suite located on the shelter deck, the top deck of the main superstructure, between the main and mizzen masts. The floor of these apartments is 2-ft (60-cm) higher than the general deck level. As a result the windows are set high enough so that ratings cannot see inside as they walk quietly by in their pumps. Ratings are in any case trained to look ahead at all times.

The sleeping quarters for the royal couple consist of two suites, each with its own bathroom and dressing room. If they want food or drink at any hour of the night they simply press a button beside the bed and a buzzer summons a white coated steward. A Royal Marine orderly is also available, stationed in the royal apartments twenty-four hours a day. The buzzer also acts as a 'panic button' in case of emergency.

Strangely, for such a palatial vessel, all the beds are single. Prince Charles had to take his own double bed on board for his honeymoon. Other royal newly-weds have not been so farsighted: Princess Anne and Captain Mark Phillips had to make do with twin beds lashed together.

Outside the royal bedroom is a wardrobe room for the Queen's clothes,

HMY. Britannia.
His Royal Highness's Sitting Room.

Above: Artist Edward Seago at work during a refuelling operation. He joined Prince Philip for his journey to the Antarctic in 1957.

Right: The glassed-in sun-veranda where the Queen enjoys her breakfast looking out over the ocean. Furniture is heavy to stop it shifting in storms. Note the mast cutting through the room.

while the corridor joining them is lined with drawings and sketches of previous yachts. A small glassed-in sitting room leads off to a glassed-in veranda where the Queen loves to have her breakfast looking out over the wide, wide ocean. Heavy bamboo furniture that won't shift in a storm is installed here. Games, records and tapes are kept here too, and there is a record player – although the Princess of Wales prefers to bring her own portable stereo with headphones on board.

Outside is the veranda deck which houses the oldest memento from royal yachts, a white and gold carved binnacle holding a compass which has been lovingly preserved from the old *Royal George*.

The binnacle is not the oldest piece on board, however. That honour goes to a naval verge presented to the Queen when she became Lord High Admiral in 1964. It was made for King Charles II's brother, the Duke of York, in 1660 for use on state occasions. Once a year it makes an appearance at the passing-out parade at Dartmouth College. The Queen herself attended this parade when Prince Andrew completed his training at Dartmouth.

Other gifts do not have quite the same pedigree, but are appreciated nonetheless. When a Torquay man sent the Queen two 200-year-old oil paintings of naval ships leaving and returning to Plymouth Sound he received a letter saying they were 'charming' and that she had ordered them to be hung in the yacht. Art sales catalogues are sent on board as regularly as racing reports for the Queen's perusal. In one catalogue she spotted an oil of the *Serapis*, the converted troop ship in which Edward VII sailed to India, and promptly sent in a bid to the London gallery and snapped it up for her personal collection on the *Britannia*.

If the Queen were to show you round the yacht no trip would be complete without a visit to the sparkling engine room nicknamed the 'Golden Rivet'. Visitors are always amazed at how clean it is. Indeed some think it is an 'exhibition' engine, the real one being housed elsewhere. Canadian Prime Minister Pierre Trudeau has been a guest on board several times, and his Press Secretary Brian Smith says: 'The memory of *Britannia* that will always stay with me is seeing that engine room. It was like looking under the bonnet of a brand new car. Other engines on ships are oily and grimy. Not *Britannia*. The Queen could eat her dinner off the floor if she wished.'

In fact cleanliness is a byword on *Britannia*, and when a rating joins he is told that the yacht must be pristine at all times. Within the smartest ship in the navy the whole atmosphere in the royal apartments is restful, the accent on comfort, not ostentation.

Discreet but charming arrangements of flowers – there are 20 in the drawing room and nine in the dining room – contribute to the light and airy mood. The standard of display is easily on a par with show levels and surprisingly they are the work of a former Royal Marine commando, Petty Officer Ian Maudsley. Normally flowers are picked from the gardens at Windsor Castle and stored in the huge refrigerators below. On long tours local flowers are bought and posies and flowers given on walkabouts used. Indeed, during her tour of British Columbia in 1983, the Queen was showered with so many bouquets that she described the yacht as 'looking like a floating flower shop'.

Royalty at play...

The pervasive air of serenity and the seemingly timeless quality of life at sea has inspired many members of the royal family to develop their artistic talents while on board. The Queen, Prince Andrew and Prince Philip all enjoy taking photographs. During his journey to Antartica, Prince Philip enjoyed photographing the birdlife, the result being a book called *Birds from Britannia*, published when he returned in 1957. Prince Andrew has developed his own talents since then, and regularly visits a photographic studio in London's

Above: the Queen and Prince Philip take time off to enjoy the fun and frivolity of a 'Crossing the Line' ceremony. The Queen captures the expressions of the hapless 'novices' on her camera just before they are ducked.

Covent Garden to develop his prints. There is even a pair of yellow rubber gloves, marked HRH in blue paint, specially for him. A book of his photos is to be published and he has also taken part in a photographic exhibition.

Landscape painter Edward Seago joined Prince Philip on his historic voyage south, and under his tuition the Prince tried his hand at sketching the scenery, and even had a go at several portraits.

Prince Charles too became an admirer and pupil of Seago. Even on his honeymoon he found time to complete two watercolours. One effort, called the 'Great Bitter Lake', was described as 'rather lame' by one critic. During another voyage up the west coast of Scotland he made up a children's story, *The Old Man of Lochnagar*, to amuse his two brothers, Princes Edward and Andrew. The tale, about an old man who lived in a dingy cave in Scotland and wanted to visit London, eventually became a best-seller, illustrated by Sir Hugh Casson.

The Princess of Wales, too, is no mean hand when it comes to putting pencil to paper. As she sat on the veranda deck, watching the icebergs in the distance, she nimbly sketched a portrait of Prince William dressed in dungarees. The picture, drawn on the back of a piece of *Britannia* notepaper, was variously described as 'sweet' and 'charming' by the critics. The sketch had a certain sentimental significance. She drew it during her tour of the eastern seaboard of Canada in 1983 while William was 3000 miles away at Kensington Palace. On the day he celebrated his first birthday with jelly and custard she was shaking hands with dignitaries at a state banquet.

She has also revived the musical tradition in the royal family, playing the piano with gusto during evening singalongs. Until Diana arrived on the royal scene, Princess Margaret was the one who kept the baby grand piano in tune.

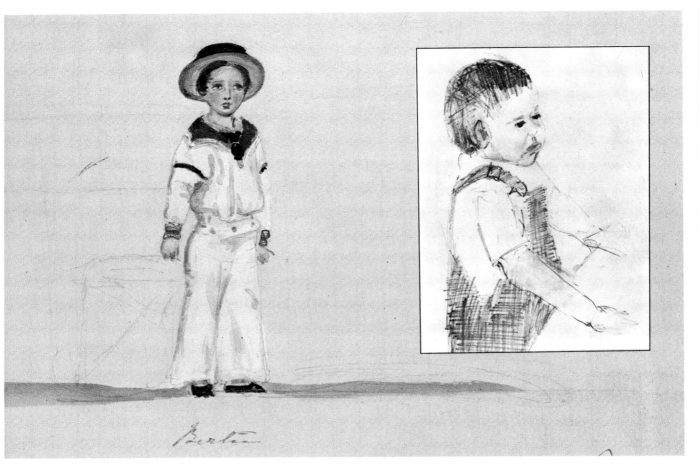

Opposite, above: Princess Elizabeth and Princess Margaret look on as the King and Queen enjoy a spot of target practice on board HMS Vanguard.

Opposite, below: George VI enjoying a game of deck quoits on the quarter deck of Vanguard. On Britannia noisy deck games are banned between two and four in the afternoon. This gives the royal family some peace and quiet, as the games deck is situated immediately above the royal apartments.

Above left: This charming portrait of Prince 'Bertie' was drawn by Queen Victoria at Falmouth in 1856 during a summer cruise on board the second Victoria and Albert.

Above right: Nearly 130 years later, a future queen, Princess Diana, drew a pencil sketch of baby Prince William while sailing off the eastern seaboard of Canada in 1983.

With a cigarette in her holder, she would play on till the early hours.

But life with the royals at sea is not all artistic amblings; sports play a large part in regal enjoyment, particularly deck quoits and hockey with everyone joining in. Prince Philip is a vigorous exponent of the ruthless art of deck hockey, as his former bodyguard Superintendent Frank Kelly remembers: 'On the long voyages we had a deck hockey league. Nobody plays deck hockey like Prince Philip. He asks no quarter and gives none.

'Bruises and cracked shins are nothing to him – given or taken. After one particularly bruising battle, the Queen told him, "You must be mad playing a game like that."'

Sir Martin Charteris, her own private secretary for twenty-seven years, was a dab hand at deck quoits. According to Patrick Lichfield, 'He was the life and soul of the party, and despite the fact that he was by no means the youngest man he nearly always beat everyone at quoits.'

To cool off there is a collapsable rubber swimming pool on the sports deck around which ratings erect canvas screens to ensure privacy. Whenever possible the Princess of Wales likes to take a daily dip.

...And at work

For the Queen, however, high jinks must take second place to her never-ending role as monarch. There is no set pattern to her day, merely a series of administrative landmarks.

She will breakfast quietly on the veranda deck with a refreshing cup of tea. Each morning the script of the 3a.m. BBC overseas service is flashed from the Admiralty to the yacht for her to read. There is also a digest of world and home news from a report sent by the Central Office of Information in London.

Above: Midnight marathon. The Queen and her private secretary Sir Martin Charteris work on into the small hours on a speech she is due to give during the state opening of Parliament in the Mauritius. The chintz furnishings were designed by Eduardo Paolozzi and Roger and Jean Nicholson.

It gives a precis of reports in British newspapers about her current tour and other doings of the royals. These give her the occasional giggle. During her tour of the South Seas she read that she was supposed to be 'furious' and in a 'rage' about her son, Prince Andrew, taking soft-porn actress Koo Stark to the Caribbean island of Mustique. In reality she thought the whole thing was highly amusing.

It was after reading such a summary, while she was off the coast of Mexico in 1983, that she gave the order to prosecute a British tabloid newspaper and a former Buckingham Palace employee who had spilled the beans about life above and below stairs.

After breakfast it is off to work in her study. There will be meetings with her private secretary and press officer to discuss fine points of detail about the next leg of the tour, and of course there is the endless stream of red boxes to be attended to. These reach her by plane, ship or helicopter no matter where she is in the world.

The red leather boxes contain Cabinet minutes, memoranda, dispatches; reports to be read, digested and in some cases signed. There are letters from ministers and ambassadors, suggested engagements, petitions from prelates or prisoners. Some have to be commented on and discussed with the relevant official. They are all dealt with conscientiously, the Queen spending three hours a day, sometimes more, on the contents.

While she is working, Prince Philip sits only a few feet away in his own office, dictating letters, sifting through correspondence, choosing future engagements. If the mood takes him he will go on to the bridge, take control for a spell, steering the yacht through the straits and narrows. During the inaugural run down the St Lawrence Seaway in 1959, 25ft (7.5m) of immaculate blue paintwork was scraped off the starboard side, and *Britannia*'s Vice Admiral Peter Dannay had to admit that it was indeed Prince Philip who had been at the helm at the time.

Paperwork is not the prerogative of the Queen and Prince Philip; all the royals have daily mountains of requests which inevitably emerge as mere molehills of acceptances. For example, Princess Anne, who is a very active President of Save the Children Fund, will spend several hours a day during the cruises around the Western Isles attending to her correspondence.

Photographer Patrick Lichfield captured one scene when *Britannia* was sailing across the Indian Ocean from the Seychelles to Mauritius. He says: 'Although it was well after midnight the Queen and her private secretary Sir Martin Charteris were still working. I believe they were preparing a speech the Queen was to give at the state opening of Parliament in Mauritius the next day. The photograph illustrates their professionalism. Not many people realize just what long hours are worked by the Queen and her staff.'

Crossing the Line

But red boxes or no, one ceremony the Queen will never miss is the slapstick fun of Crossing the Line, when the royal yacht sails over the Equator. The fun and games began in 1791, and the ceremony has been retained in its original form ever since. A typical entry in the yacht's log reads: '0916. Neptune's court in session. 1030. Neptune's court in chaos.' *Britannia* usually stops her engines at about sunset the day before she is due to cross the Equator. From behind a screen rigged up on deck King Neptune's messengers emerge to deliver an address of welcome to the ship now 'entering Neptune's domains'.

At the same time they summon all those who have never crossed before to appear before Neptune's court at a certain time on the following day. Then King Neptune and Queen Amphitrite make their appearance, attended by the Court officials consisting of the Clerk of the Court, doctor, barber, police and the bears. After a ceremonial parade round the upper deck they take their places at the court. The novices – those who haven't crossed the Equator before – enter, and one by one take a seat where they are lathered and shaved by the barber before being given a pill by the doctor. (When George V heard that his son, later Edward VIII, had taken part in this undignified procedure he warned him, 'Remember your station.') While this is in progress the seat is tipped up, throwing its helpless victims into the yacht's canvas swimming pool, where they are ducked unmercifully by the bears. The police search out

Above and right: Prepare for a ducking. Prince Philip, protected by a butcher's apron (above), takes his place as the 'assistant barber' during a 'Crossing the Line' ceremony on board the SS Gothic during the Queen's Commonwealth tour in 1954. During another ceremony on the Indian Ocean (right), the Queen watches the good clean fun.

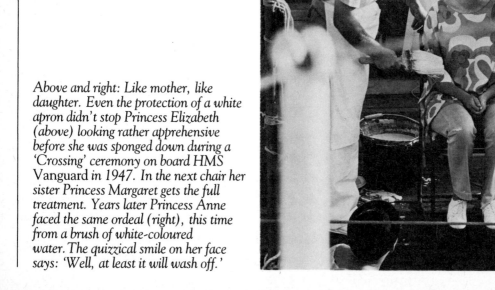

Above and right: Like mother, like daughter. Even the protection of a white apron didn't stop Princess Elizabeth (above) looking rather apprehensive before she was sponged down during a 'Crossing' ceremony on board HMS Vanguard in 1947. In the next chair her sister Princess Margaret gets the full treatment. Years later Princess Anne faced the same ordeal (right), this time from a brush of white-coloured water. The quizzical smile on her face says: 'Well, at least it will wash off.'

all those who try to escape, and at the end of this ceremony the Clerk of the Court issues each initiate with a certificate proving he has become a subject of King Neptune.

Even during wartime the tradition continues. Prince Andrew was hunted down by the ship's police on HMS *Invincible* and soundly ducked as the Task Force sailed to the Falklands.

When the Queen and Prince Philip were on board SS *Gothic* on the outward journey of their historic world cruise in 1954, Philip took part with gusto. His nose was red with greasepaint, and with a blue and white butcher's apron flapping round his legs he had a splash-happy time, throwing luckless novices into the pool. The Queen filmed the crazy carry-on but escaped a ducking herself on the grounds that she had undergone the ordeal during the 1947 cruise to South Africa on board the battleship *Vanguard*. Then she and Princess Margaret had aprons tied round to stop their skirts from getting too wet while their faces were rubbed with a wet sponge. Not quite the full-blown ceremony, but it gave a lot of harmless fun to the watching ship's company.

During the Silver Wedding tour of the South Seas Patrick Lichfield snapped the Queen laughing at his discomfiture when he was caught and ducked.

Right: The Queen watches with obvious enjoyment as her cousin, the photographer Lord Lichfield, is first covered in shaving cream then ducked by the 'bears'. He recalled: 'I received my summons from Lord Plunket who said, "I hope you've got an old suit with you because you're for it."'

Above: A dazzling display of diamonds and medals, as the Queen and Prince Philip join the Sultan of Oman for a group photograph before an official banquet on board during a state visit in 1979.

Traditions and formalities

As the Lord High Admiral, the Queen is technically the highest ranking officer on board *Britannia*, and it is to her that the ship's captain, Rear Admiral Paul Greening, reports daily. The admiral, who is part of the Queen's Household, discusses problems on board the yacht, possible route changes and other fine tuning that is part and parcel of royal tours. In addition there is a special royal charthouse below the bridge fitted with a radar viewer, instruments to record speed and distance travelled and a 10-ft (3-m) wide map of the world showing the tour route in detail. From here, the Queen may issue signals to escort ships or reply to greetings from those saluting her.

When the Queen is at sea in between tour stops, the need for elaborate state banquets on board is dispensed with. However, there are still certain formalities to be observed, certain traditions upheld.

One such is the twenty-six piece Royal Marine band which serenades the Queen around the world. The band is paraded at 8a.m. for the ceremony of hoisting colours. During lunch and dinner they play in an adjoining room to the royal diners, regaling them with everything from waltzes and classical tunes to military marches and pop.

The band is a specially selected section of the band of the Commander in Chief Naval Home Command. It is taken on board for all important overseas

Above and right: Dining in style.
The dining room (above) can seat fifty-
six guests. It takes three hours to set the
table; the placing of every knife, fork and
spoon is measured meticulously by ruler.
Every guest gets a menu in French
(right) to take home as a souvenir of a
night to remember.
The dining room also doubles as a
cinema. The Queen and Prince Philip
always sit in the front row, members of
the Household and guests behind. 'No
one ever dares to walk up and sit next to
the Queen', says one guest. 'It is rather
like going to a church where the first
three rows are empty because you want
to avoid the vicar's gaze. If the film is a
comedy it's hard to know whether to
laugh at the funny bits. The result is a
series of nervous titters.'

EꞮꞮR

H.M.Y. BRITANNIA

Saumon Suédoise

Perdreau Rôti Maréchale
Salade

Profiteroles Glacées au Chocolat

Mardi, le 22 février, 1977

Auckland

tours under the command of a Director of Music. It comprises eight violins, one viola, two cellos, one double bass, two horns, flute, clarinet and oboe and, as all the players are capable of performing on wind instruments, it is quickly transformed into a ceremonial or concert band for outdoor events. At one time a fiddler was always carried on board a royal yacht, a survivor of the sailing-ship days when music was provided for weighing the anchor, hoisting the sail and so on. Practising on board is a problem, as the strict rule is for noise to be kept to a minimum. To avoid annoying the royals, the band uses a space in the recreation room in the forward section of the ship – as far away from the royal apartments as is practicable.

The musical programme always appears on the dining table with the menus, each diner receiving a copy. They are decided before *Britannia* ever sets sail from Portsmouth, as are the guest lists.

During state visits the guests on board are usually the Prime Minister or President of the host country and his family. Often the British Foreign Secretary is a guest, staying in one of the seventeen guest cabins on the main deck which also accommodate the Household. Lunch is a quiet affair and dinner a little more formal. Guests gather in the anteroom and chat to courteous officers from the yacht who act as their hosts until the Queen arrives. Conversation, when the Queen is present, can cover a considerable range of topics. When Susan Crosland was on board she was given a celebrated piece of advice from the Queen on how to stand for hours without tiring. 'One plants one's feet apart like this,' the Queen told her, hoisting up her skirts. 'Always keep them parallel. Make sure your weight is evenly distributed. That's all there is to it.'

Dress depends on climate and is carefully specified to guests before they come aboard. For example, in the tropics the correct evening dress on *Britannia* is white mess dress, though on occasions when at sea this is relaxed to Red Sea Rig – an open-necked dress shirt with cummerbund and dress trousers. After aperitifs have been served the dining room doors are opened on a pre-arranged signal and the guests proceed through, a lady on the arm of each gentleman. Normally the kitchens below cater for about sixteen guests, and members of the Royal Household, and for thirty staff. Only the guests and members of the Household eat with the Royal Family. Naturally guests remain standing until the royal hosts are seated.

Grace is not said and ashtrays are only brought to the table at the end of the meal. After-dinner conversation continues in the drawing room. Depending on who is present for dinner everyone may decide to watch a film in the dining room. Modern twin projectors with an automatic reel change operate from the servery to fill a wide screen, and about forty feature-length films are brought on board at the start of a tour. Anything starring Barbra Streisand gets the seal of approval from Prince Andrew and Prince Charles.

During the course of the day, if there is a secluded bay or island nearby, the yacht may heave to so that the royal party can disembark for an evening stroll or an afternoon barbecue. It is all a question of time and tide and, although they wait for no man, the yacht's navigator does his best to make sure they work in tandem for the Queen's pleasure.

Opposite above: The Queen walks from her rooms on to the veranda deck for a ceremony of welcome in Fiji, where she was presented with a necklace of shark's teeth.

Opposite below: The Queen performs an investiture during a visit to the Bahamas. The knighting stool is kept in the drawing room. The royal yacht is a travelling palace and discharges the many functions of a royal residence.

Below: Prince Andrew joins his parents in a discussion of the details of the day's journey. All members of the royal family take an active interest in the day-to-day running of the yacht.

3

HOLIDAY HOME –
COWES AND SCOTLAND

*'Sailing on a sunny day, with a fresh
breeze blowing... is the nearest thing to heaven
anyone will ever get on this earth.'*

PRINCESS ANNE

If horse racing is the sport of kings then sailing is the sport of princes, and Cowes Week its crowning glory. For more than 150 years this sleepy town on the Isle of Wight has been the annual August playground for European royalty. It is a colourful scene: small boats, large boats, scores of yachts scudding across the Solent, their sails billowing and blossoming in the breeze. For the last thirty years the royal yacht *Britannia* has dominated the scene, her colourful dress flags fluttering gaily. The thousands who flock there every year have the chance to see the royal family having fun. Prince Philip at the helm of the tiny Racing Fifteen *Cowslip*, Princess Anne and Prince Edward crewing on one of the bigger yachts, Prince Charles in a black wetsuit splashing about on a windsurfer, or Prince Andrew, a pretty girl by his side, going for a spin in a speedboat.

Previous page: A typical Cowes scene. The royal yacht is in the background while Superstar *and* Marionette *vie for positions during the Admiral's Cup race.*

Above: Prince Edward with a 'yachtie' at the helm of Spanish Lady.

Opposite: At the helm. Prince Philip, who has been a Cowes regular for more than thirty years, on board the Yeoman class yacht which he races with varying degrees of success.

Even when princes play, though, certain time-honoured rituals have to be observed, for tradition plays a crucial part in a Cowes holiday. This dates back to the early nineteenth century, when the Prince Regent heard about the delights of a newly founded yachting club in Cowes, and in 1817 forsook his favourite seaside resort of Brighton and joined in the fun. As a result the word 'royal' was added to its name and Society flocked to watch.

In 1826 came the first race for a cup, but a free-for-all developed between competing yachtsmen when two boats collided. A year later the inauguration of a King's Cup produced celebrations described by the local papers as 'continuing until the blacksmith of night struck the anvil of morn'. British and foreign monarchs alike made their annual pilgrimage to Cowes, and Queen Victoria and Prince Albert particularly loved the event.

But while the Queen loved to watch the sailing, it was the Prince of Wales, later Edward VII, who, in 1863, set the stamp of glamour on the event. It was a welcome end to his hectic London season, and he also found it useful as an away-from-court holiday with his current love, the music-hall actress Lily Langtry. For several years running she visited a small cottage opposite West Cowes Castle, home of 'the Squadron', as the yacht club was called. Fashionable society arrived in droves to catch a glimpse of 'the Lily' and His Royal Highness.

The Prince gave a considerable impetus to yacht racing not only by his patronage, but also by his enthusiastic participation. For many years he owned a number of racing yachts, the last and best known being the cutter *Britannia* which, in a career stretching from 1893 to 1935, collected 231 first prizes. Edward loved this elegant craft, which was 'as handy and lively as a kitten', and on his death it passed to his son George V, who was equally enamoured with her. Sir Philip Hunloke, the King's Racing Master, said of the relationship between yacht and royal master, 'Aboard the *Britannia*, the King was like a schoolboy home for a holiday. He loved the old yacht; he enjoyed winning but was a splendid loser.'

For the last thirty years Prince Philip has nobly carried on the Cowes tradition, but he is the first to admit that a Dragon Class boat given as a wedding present and the tiny *Cowslip*, kept on board *Britannia*, are not in the same league as the old *Britannia*. As he says, 'No one could bring themselves to look upon an overgrown dinghy and a class boat with a three-man crew as royal yachts, certainly not as direct successors to the majestic old *Britannia*.'

Prince Philip found a kindred spirit in the late boatbuilder Uffa Fox, bluff, down-to-earth, and outspoken. They spent many days in each other's company during Cowes Week. Competitively, Prince Philip was an excellent helmsman – 'seldom out of the picture in a race', as Uffa once said. But he has also had his share of mishaps with Uffa. On one occasion he came close to serious injury when a heavy crane boom collapsed while he was trying to lift *Cowslip* out of the water. The boat had gone over after another competitor had come too close. Uffa and the Prince had to be towed in by a nearby yachting photographer. The Prince helped to fix slings to the boat to bring it on to the landing stage. As the waterlogged Racing Fifteen was about to be lifted out the combined weight of water and boat ripped the crane from the wall, and it crashed down just two feet away from the Prince. He merely shrugged off the mishap, however.

Britannia, star of Cowes

For him, and other members of the royal family, Cowes Week is the first stage in an annual holiday routine on *Britannia* that takes in a cruise round the Western Isles of Scotland and finishes in the peace and privacy of Balmoral. Like other royal yachts before her, *Britannia* plays an essential part in the royal

Above: Spit and polish. The yacht's hull being painted in its unique high-gloss blue paint in preparation for the Silver Jubilee Review off Spithead.

Below: Oops, a splash of white after a painting accident had tourists flocking to take a closer look.

summer break. She is always given a fresh lick of paint in her home port of Portsmouth to prepare her for Cowes Week, and when the yacht ties up to a buoy in the Solent, crewmen apply the finishing touches. (In 1971, when a crewman fell off his supporting plank whilst working, and left a huge scar of white paint on the hull, boat trips were organized to take a look.)

If she has not been used for some time, *Britannia* will go through her paces in the Channel to try out her machinery and adjust her compasses. But once tied up, work will begin to make her ship-shape. The royal barges are hoisted on their davits, covers come off the furniture in the royal apartments, and a secure telephone link to the mainland is established. By now a cabin plan will have arrived from the Master of the Household showing the names of the royal guests and the cabins they will occupy. Princess Alexandra, Angus Ogilvy and their children are welcome regulars, as is Princess Margaret's daughter, Lady Sarah Armstrong Jones. It is a time too to bring girlfriends on board, for as one among many guests aboard *Britannia*, they can merge in with the others. The Princess of Wales visited Cowes in 1980 before her engagement and had a marvellous time, exploring the yacht and watching Prince Charles windsurf. The story goes that she caused gales of innocent mirth when she upset his windsurfer and gave him a ducking.

The day before the royals arrive, the royal servants, including valets, kitchen staff, dressers and secretaries settle in. As the visit to Cowes is a private one, ceremony is dispensed with as far as possible, but when the Queen and Prince Philip arrive, she is piped aboard, the officers standing in a single line facing outboard, the ship's company mustered at divisions. After the officers are presented, the company are all fallen out and get on with their duties.

On the rare occasions that the Queen is on board at Cowes, twenty-one-gun salutes are fired by the escort ship, shore batteries, and the Royal Yacht Squadron at Cowes. One year the cannon in front of the Squadron went missing. The culprits were old seadog Uffa Fox and Prince Philip. It was found a few miles away and discreetly replaced. On another famous occasion, the devilish duo decided to re-enact the Battle of Trafalgar inside the Royal London Sailing Club with small cannons reputed to have been on *Victory*. The result, still chuckled over at the Club, was a few smashed windows and a bill for the damage.

Balls, banquets, banter and bonhomie are the stuff of Cowes Week. One night a fancy-dress party at a country-house; another, a light-hearted dinner with yachting chums on board *Britannia*.

Another example of Uffa's jovial nature concerned Prince Charles, whom he taught to sail. To press home to the Prince just how behind he had been after coming in ninth out of thirty starters in one race in *Cowslip*, Uffa appeared wearing a nightshirt and nightcap, and carrying a candle.

Princess Anne is a great fan of *Britannia*. She loves the informality of life on board and especially looks forward to Cowes Week, as her birthday, on August 15th, often falls during the week. Many is the party she has enjoyed on board, the silver-grey carpet of the Drawing Room unrolled to reveal a parquet floor just right for dancing, and on warm nights, an awning is erected overhead on the shelter deck.

Murmurs of protest were heard in some quarters when the royal yacht became a floating discotheque for her twenty-first birthday celebrations, with 120 specially invited guests dancing until the early hours. The day before, anti-monarchist MP Willie Hamilton had visited the yacht after criticizing the cost of a refit. As he later commented, 'We were told that any drinks would have to be paid for. Quite right too. The very next day Princess Anne was having her twenty-first birthday party on board. Who paid for the drinks then?'

Left: King George V at the helm of his beloved 'J' class yacht Britannia during Cowes week in 1924. He never took command during a race, though, deferring to the skill of Sir Philip Hunloke.

Below left: The Giles cartoon is spot on. Prince Philip does get very angry when fellow yachtsmen sail too close for a look at the royal sailor.

Below: Prince Philip is an aggressive competitor, seen here racing his Bloodhound for the first time during the Britannia Challenge Cup in 1962.

"I know he don't like you taking his picture while he's racing—but I didn't know he'd got a polo mallet on board."

Right: Sail on the Solent. These two pictures illustrate the timeless quality of royal yachting.
The cutter Britannia in full sail (above) is captured on canvas by artist Norman Wilkinson. King George V, normally a stickler for accuracy, was delighted with the picture but he asked for one small change. He requested that the buoy be moved a little nearer the yacht so that it would appear to be making a tighter and more seamanlike turn. Mr Wilkinson agreed.
Prince Philips's yawl Bloodhound is seen here at Cowes (below). This ocean-going craft was also used to explore Norwegian fjords and inlets on the west coast of Scotland.

Opposite: All the royals have a love of the sea.
Prince Charles gets his leg pulled by Uffa Fox (top left) who came down to the quayside in a nightshirt and carrying a candle to rub home the point that the Prince had come ninth out of thirty starters on board Cowslip.
During a summer cruise on Britannia the younger royals (top right) show off their semaphore. The clear message from Prince Andrew, Prince Edward and Princess Margaret's children, Viscount Linley and Lady Sarah Armstrong Jones, is: 'We're having fun.'
Princess Anne (below) appears in a reflective mood as she sails with Lord Burghersh. She once wrote in her school magazine: 'If it is blowing then sailing becomes a fight . . . you become part of your ship, testing your skill, not against anyone else's but against nature . . .'

When they were youngsters, Uffa Fox had taught Princess Anne and her brother Charles to sail, and they were frequent visitors at his Cowes home, playing gleefully amongst the assortment of lobster pots, fishing nets and trophies that decorated the house. One evening during Cowes Week was always set aside for a visit by the royals to his Commodore's House for dinner and a singsong round the piano. As a result of the time spent at Uffa's, at the tender age of nine Anne could coil rope correctly and fold tarpaulin.

Prince Charles also has a soft spot for Cowes – and the royal yacht. Indeed, his early voyages on board inspired him to go to sea. As a toddler he fostered friendships with crew members and was delighted when he was given a real seaman's hat. At first he wouldn't take it off, and later it had pride of place on his bedroom wall at Buckingham Palace, together with a picture of *Britannia*. On another occasion, he roamed through the company's sleeping quarters

Above: Up, up and away. Prince Charles enjoys windsurfing on the Solent, watched by cameramen waiting for a slip.

early one morning and ended up with a right royal rollicking from a notoriously grumpy matelot. For a lark, other ratings had told the Prince to wake the slumbering sailor by thumping him as he slept in his hammock. He did so, but suddenly there was a great roar and a hand reached down to grab the small royal. 'Don't ever do that again, laddie, or you'll never grow up to be king,' snapped the ill-tempered sailor.

But the royal children have always had a free and easy relationship with the ratings, and the Queen insists that they are never given preferential treatment. One rating described them as 'Wonderful kids, charming and unaffected. One time they went to the NAAFI shop to buy sweets. They queued up like everybody else.'

Ratings are often given the job of looking after younger royal children, and one man, known by everyone as 'Mr Yacht' has seen them all grow up. He is the ship's coxswain, Ellis Norrell – the Queen calls him Norrie – who has been with *Britannia* since three days before she was commissioned. He helped teach the royal youngsters to water-ski – driving the speed boat for their trial-runs.

It was no doubt Charles' many visits to *Britannia* which fired his interest in the sea. Whilst still at school, he sent his parents a crayon drawing of *Bloodhound*, Prince Philip's boat.

For many years, until she was sold in 1969, the yawl *Bloodhound* was a family favourite. Charles, Anne and Prince Philip spent many a lazy day sailing through the Crinian canal or simply exploring coves and creeks, enjoying picnics on isolated beaches and walks ashore. They often had harmless fun by knocking on the doors of crofter's cottages asking for water. The game was to remain unrecognized for as long as possible.

In her school magazine at Benenden, Princess Anne set down her feelings about sailing:

'Sailing on a sunny day, with a fresh breeze blowing . . . is the nearest thing to heaven anyone will ever get on this earth – certainly the nearest I will ever get. . . . The silence is blissful after you switch off the engine. The only sound is the rush of the water, relaxing and hypnotic, the gentle creak of the rigging and occasional flap of a lazy sail. It gives me an utterly detached sensation that I have only otherwise experienced on a galloping horse.'

During Cowes Week there is a steady stream of visitors to *Britannia* paying courtesy calls. Usually they enter by the port after gangway ladder and enter their names in the visitors' book at the entry port. Similarly, tradition has it that the royals visit the escort vessel, paying calls to the captain's cabin and the officer's mess. Then there are visits to some of the more exotic boats on show: a Russian hydrofoil one year, a replica of Sir Francis Drake's *Golden Hind* another. During the visit to the *Hind*, Prince Philip and Prince Andrew astounded everyone when they went 'ape' on board. As they toured the tiny vessel, moored near *Britannia*, they reached the between decks, a space just 4ft 6in (1.4-m) high. First Philip started swinging his arms and making grunting noises, and Andrew followed suit. 'It was hilarious', said one crew member, 'real holiday high jinks'.

And it's not just the royals who let their hair down after the year's round of strenuous public engagements. The ratings too have their fun. One year two revelling crewmen were disciplined when they three times broke into a house-party where a bevy of blonde beauties were sunbathing topless. The police were called and subsequently Prince Charles apologized on their behalf. Later, while windsurfing, he saw the girls, covered up this time, and said, a twinkle in his eye, 'Oh, so you're the topless lot. Why aren't you topless now?'

If Sunday Service is held on board, it takes place in the royal apartments,

Above and left: All hands on deck. King George V (above) enjoys a day's cruising with his friends on Britannia, and (left) the crew handle the yacht's 10,000 square feet of sail. The sentimental King had a lifelong love-affair with this glorious lady of sail. He was determined that she should not end up as a museum piece. One of his last wishes was to send the yacht to a watery grave. So on the afternoon of 8 July 1936 the yacht, a garland of flowers laid gently on her stern, was towed out of Marvin's Yard for her last resting place. An explosive charge was attached and Britannia was taken out to deep waters off the Isle of Wight and sunk.

with all the Household present. The Royal Marine band provides the music and the yacht's captain, Rear Admiral Paul Greening, takes the service. Prince Philip may read the lesson. This seldom occurs during Cowes Week however as the Royal Family traditionally attend the Cowes Church.

To the isles

Britannia usually leaves Cowes on a Monday, with little ceremony, and is under way before 8a.m. followed by the attendant destroyer. And then it is off for the isles and inlets of the Scottish west coast, taking on board the Queen and other members of the royal family, normally at Southampton. Nothing is too much trouble during this seaborne saunter up to the Scottish coast. One year the royal yacht anchored at Holyhead for an hour, simply to post some letters, and local coastguard officials were warned of her arrival shortly beforehand. It was on another cruise that the Prince of Wales first set foot on that principality. At Milford Haven a launch took him to the beach for a paddle and to make sandcastles.

During the cruise the royal yacht will go out of its way to seek out the secluded stretches along the west coast of Scotland. This is a holiday tradition dating back to Queen Victoria's time. And George VI, when he sailed for Balmoral, would stop at his famous Duke of York's Camp where boys from working-class and public school backgrounds mixed in a unique and unusual recreational experiment. When he arrived, he was borne ashore through the waves from an open royal boat on the bare shoulders of his young friends.

For the present royal family, slacks, sneakers, sandals and T-shirts are the usual mode of dress during the Queen's holiday cruise, and she loves this family time so much that she has issued several Christmas cards showing the family at leisure on board.

The Queen and Prince Philip occupy the royal suite; the royal children, Andrew, Edward, Princess Anne and her two children Zara and Peter the guest cabins on the main deck. These days Prince Charles and Princess Diana usually fly up to Balmoral later. As far as meals go, breakfast is a casual, serve-yourself affair, and lunch is informal, but afternoon tea at 4.30p.m. is quite a ceremony in itself. 'In our family, everything stops for tea', Prince Charles once said. 'I have never known a family so addicted to it.' The Queen is something of a fusspot about getting the brew just right, using a Darjeeling blend. 'Such a cosy meal,' she says, as she relaxes with a refreshing cuppa in her private sitting room, a tray of egg and cress sandwiches and muffins by her side. Dinner is the main meal of the day, when everyone joins the Queen and Prince Philip at table. And then there are the barbecues...

Whatever the weather, the royals relish their barbecues and picnics on any of the many isolated beaches of the Scottish Isles. Prince Charles freely admits he got his own taste for barbecues on these trips, where his father is the Master of Ceremonies. One year they stopped by at the Isle of Uist, for a feast upon a 'bleak and totally solitary islet, sadly disrupted by millions of midges.' Uffa Fox was with the royal party, including Prince Philip's German relatives, when they were ferried ashore for another picnic lunch. Uffa's biographer, June Dixon, takes up the story:

'Relaxed after an agreeable meal, the grown ups were sitting around idly chatting of this and that, leaving the children to play and let off steam, when the then very young Prince Charles began teasing his mother by aiming small, round, hard pellets in her direction. The Queen responded in kind, and within seconds a friendly battle was raging as various members of the royal family pelted one another enthusiastically with rabbit-droppings.'

'Picnics to the royals are as banquets to the rest of us,' said one royal servant. The royal barbecues have even impressed world leaders who have

Opposite: Highland Fling.
The royal holidaymakers come ashore at Applecross (above) for an informal visit – and there's a rare sight of the Queen in trousers.
Will ye no' come back again? To the sound of pipes, the Queen, Prince Philip and Princess Margaret leave Dunvegan Castle slipway during a visit to Skye in 1956 (below left).
Princess Anne and Prince Charles show off their kilts as they step smartly ashore at Stornoway (below right).

stayed on board the royal yacht as guests. The former Australian Prime Minister John Gorton enjoyed one such feast during the Queen's Bicentenary visit in 1970. And like so many other beach banquets it ended in fun and frivolity. He recalls that he nearly ended up throwing the Queen in the sea:

'The royal yacht had anchored near one of the islands off the Great Barrier Reef. It was very civilized. Half the crew went ashore before us to spray everything so there were no sand-flies or mosquitoes. The chef started grilling on spits and handing food around in a really de-luxe picnic. It started off quietly but developed into a lot of fun. Somebody decided everybody should be thrown into the water.

'Princess Anne was thrown in and then Prince Philip. I was sitting next to Her Majesty and I was about to throw her in, but I looked at her, and it was something about the way she looked at me . . . Anyway, she was the only one who stayed dry.'

The icy North Atlantic, however, is hardly the place for impromptu duckings, although even when the royals go ashore informally, all sorts of preparations have to be made. The Scotland Yard detectives go ahead to 'recce' the beach. However secluded it may seem, it's best to be sure. At least in the Western Isles, they are safe from the prying lenses of cameramen. Fleet Street rarely comes this far north – too chancy and costly – and the local press has an informal agreement to leave the royals alone on holiday.

Then the royal barge loaded with royals arrives at the barbecue site, and for several hours they are on their own, a detective watching from either end of the bay. As one former royal servant says, 'They don't mind cooking and serving themselves, but clearing up is out.' In between the barbecues and the scuba diving, the water-skiing and the deck-hockey, there is the occasional

Below: Flags at bay. Britannia, dressed overall, waits serenely while the Queen visits a paper mill at Fort William.

Above: Prince Andrew, sporting a beard, gets a kiss from the Queen Mother when he and other members of the royal family arrive at Scrabster harbour to spend the day at her Castle of Mey.

Right: Prince Charles finds peace and relaxation with a spot of rowing away from the madding crowd. The isolated coves and inlets which Britannia winkles out give the royal family a chance to indulge their favourite pastimes in private.

Above: August 1967. The royal family set sail from Southampton for their annual cruise. The trip could have been delayed by striking dockers, but they postponed a union meeting to let the royals get under way.

formal visit to be fitted in. It may be Northern Ireland one year, one of the many Western Isles the next. It was after one such visit, when they were toddlers – this time to the Isle of Man – that Prince Charles and Princess Anne were allowed to stay up until seven o'clock to watch a firework display through the portholes.

Occasionally, the odd drama livens up the leisurely pace of the holiday cruise. One year the Queen had to be hoisted aboard the royal yacht from the Isle of Skye because the sea was too rough. During another storm, *Britannia* went to the rescue of a Lynx helicopter which had ditched in the sea. But she was too late – the pilot was lost. On another cruise, the Queen held a brief Privy Council meeting to give the go-ahead to the marriage between two aristocrats, technically in line to the throne. Even on holiday, state work is never forgotten.

Heading on round the coast, *Britannia* anchors in the early morning at Scrabster harbour, near Thurso. Here the Queen Mother has her Scottish retreat, a romantic but isolated home, the castle of Mey, a stone's throw from the beach. Every year they disembark and arrive at the granite steps of Scrabster harbour, the local harbourmaster making sure everything goes according to plan.

On the harbour road the Queen Mother pulls up in her black Daimler with her lady-in-waiting, Ruth, Lady Fermoy – Princess Diana's grandmother – standing nearby. The royals disembark from the royal barge and make their way up the steps at 11a.m. sharp – the ritual never varies. In 1983, Prince Andrew was sporting a beard, grown during a hiking trip through the wilds of Canada.' Oh I do like your beard,' the beaming Queen Mother told him. Rather sheepishly Andrew gave her a peck on the cheek. It's a family reunion, watched by a thousand loyal locals, many of whom the Queen Mother and the Queen know by name.

Above: August 1976. Refreshed and relaxed, the royal family arrive at Aberdeen for their summer break at Balmoral, the Queen's Highland home.

After lunch at the castle, followed by a walk through the grounds and high tea, the royal party embark for Aberdeen. There follows a little-known family ceremony – virtually impossible to photograph – that truly marks the start of the royal summer holiday. As *Britannia* steams away, the Queen Mother always sends up huge multi-coloured rockets from the turrets of her castle for a dramatic farewell. As the rockets burst into the evening sky, the staff wave big white sheets from the battlements. In return *Britannia* sends up flares, scorching streaks of white light into the sky. The excitement over, everyone looks forward to the arrival at Aberdeen and those long days on the grouse moors of the vast Balmoral estate.

Usually the royal yacht arrives at Aberdeen harbour at 6a.m. in what is known as 'silent order'. The engines are cut and she docks as quietly as possible so as not to wake the Queen. (In the past, night construction workers have been told to take a break until the Queen has risen.) By early morning, a small crowd is waiting to greet the royals, often diverted by the sight of a crewman touching up paintwork on the hull. One year, an American tourist watched in awe as preparations were made to disembark. He saw the Royal Marine band go on deck, and watched open-mouthed as, dead on eight, they started playing a tune from the hit musical *The King and I*. 'What are they doing that for?' he asked a bearded Scottish photographer. 'They play every morning before the Queen gets up,' the photographer replied. 'Gee,' was the response. 'That must be the most expensive alarm clock in the world!' Both had fallen into the trap of thinking that the band plays to wake the Queen. In fact it is paraded at eight in the morning for the ceremony of hoisting colours and assembles on the forecastle for the express reason of not disturbing Her Majesty.

And so from bed on board to Balmoral, leaving *Britannia* to breeze back to base at Portsmouth . . . and the world's most extraordinary holiday cruise is over for another year.

THE POWERS BEHIND
THE SCENES

*'A posting on board Britannia
is the most glamorous in the Navy.'*

ROYAL YACHT RATING

On a grey misty morning in Halifax, Nova Scotia, *Britannia* lies tied up by the wide, tarmac quayside. At 9.45a.m. sharp a murmur of recognition comes from the patiently waiting crowd. Prince Charles, in his usual grey suit, and the Princess of Wales, in a violet blue outfit, emerge from the royal apartments and walk steadily down to the stepped royal gangway. Before she steps onto the deep red carpet Diana hesitates for a second as if bracing herself for the day ahead. Then, with a quick glance down, she starts the 20-ft (6-m) walk from ship to shore, occasionally gripping the varnished handrail.

At the bottom a squabble of photographers – the 'Nikon choir' as they are known – waits to serenade her. The Princess smiles and shakes hands. A routine entrance, another royal day off to a flawless start.

Above: Rolling out the red carpet. Workmen complete the plans for the ceremonial welcome for the Prince and Princess of Wales during a visit to Charlottetown, Prince Edward Island, in 1983.

Previous page: Ahoy there! A Britannia yachtsman puts the finishing touches to the royal crest on the yacht's bow.

But you never know; a too-steep slope, an awkward slip and the unexpected can become the picture of the year. However, there is a small army of people who do their best to ensure that the unexpected never happens. For every step the Princess of Wales takes down that gangway, an ocean of paperwork has gone before her. In the words of one *Britannia* officer, a royal landing 'must look right'. As the yacht's current captain, Rear Admiral Paul Greening, put it, 'If you are taking part in a ceremonial arrival you don't want the Queen to have to cling to the rail because the gangway is so steep. It detracts from the dignity of the occasion.'

Rules and practice have the whole operation down to a fine art. The tide must be such that the slope of the gangway is never steeper than 15 degrees. When later during that same tour in 1983 the Princess of Wales disembarked from the 40-ft (12-m) long barge to go to church in the little town of St Andrews by Sea, New Brunswick, a 'recce' party from the royal yacht had gone before to make certain that the quay steps were not too steep or slippery for the Princess. It is detail like that, laid down and logged, that is the bread and butter for that elite band of men who crew the royal yacht.

Before *Britannia* ever sets sail from Portsmouth, Rear Admiral Greening will have teamed up with officials from Buckingham Palace to look over the royal route. A vital consideration is to ensure that prospective harbours are suitable for the royal yacht, bearing in mind such details as water depth, and jetties and local hazards. Prince Charles' plan that *Britannia* could be anchored near Caenarvon Castle for his Investiture had to be scrapped when it was discovered that a smaller training ship had run aground there.

Above: Flag day. Britannia docks on a grey Saturday morning in San Diego on the first leg of the Queen's momentous Californian tour. In the background, a huge American flag on top of a local bank makes a neat contrast with the Union Jack.

'We also have to make sure that *Britannia* is not overlooked when we dock,' says the Rear Admiral. 'It's essential both from a security point of view, and that when the Queen has come back from a heavy day she has privacy and peace. If she wants to take the air she doesn't want thousands of people staring at her. It's important that she can relax in private surroundings.'

The Yachtsmen's task is to make sure that everything goes like clockwork and works precisely, and the royals get their rest. When things go wrong – which is rare – they make front-page news. During an earlier trip to Canada in 1964 the Queen noticed a slight warning movement from the gangplank as she was about to walk up. 'I'm not going up there, it moved,' she said firmly. Seconds later the gangway parted from its platform with a jolting thud and the efforts of a dozen straining sailors could do little to stop it tipping crazily into the air. The Queen, splendid in a turquoise evening gown, and Prince Philip stood shivering in the night air as sailors worked frantically to secure the errant gangway. When an officer smartly reported that all was well, Prince Philip remarked briskly, 'All right, let's go up before anything else happens.' An inquiry was launched that night and as the yacht sailed away from the dock, the Royal Marine band played 'Wish Me Luck As You Wave Me Goodbye' – a cheeky bit of inter-Service one-upmanship.

But the men will never make a drama out of a crisis. In 1975 when the Queen Mother was returning from a tour of the Channel Isles, she was coming ashore on board the royal barge to a waiting pontoon in Portsmouth harbour. As she stepped on to the pontoon her handbag slipped out of her grasp down a small gap between barge and pontoon. Quick as a flash, the royal barge officer

Lieutenant Hugh Slade flung himself to the ground and just managed to retrieve the royal handbag before it disappeared into the Solent. As a token of her gratitude the Queen Mother sent him a pair of cufflinks and a hand-written letter thanking him for 'the finest salvage job ever carried out by the Royal Navy'.

The ship's company

The ship's company pride themselves on getting things right . . . and quickly. For that, planning is the password to success. After the 'recce' has taken place, the really fine detail has to be worked out. Months before the Queen was due to sail down the St Lawrence in the summer of 1984, the yacht's navigating officer was having sleepless nights worrying about how he could squeeze the ship through lock gates where he only had 5-ft (1.5-m) to spare.

Before *Britannia* leaves port, her route has been carefully mapped out to the metre. Local tides, details of currents, local light and buoy lists have all been carefully examined. Each day the Admiralty expects an unclassified message from *Britannia* saying exactly where she is and what she is up to. Admiralty papers for King George VI's tour of Canada on board HMS *Repulse* before the war give some idea of the detailed planning that takes place:

Leaving Portsmouth at 1600 BST on 8th May 1939. Time on journey 6½ days

Ship must steam a) 21 knots, making good 20.2 knots for 98 hours . . . 1,980 miles

b) 17 knots making good 15 knots for 62 hours.

The voyage has to be split up into sections, as given above, so as to reach the eastern edge of the probable ice danger zone in latitude 47N 45W at daylight and pass through probable ice track at high speed during daylight hours.

When Prince Charles and the Princess of Wales visited the eastern seaboard of Canada forty-four years later, *Britannia* still had a detailed route planned. This time they had radar and could sail through 'iceberg alley' with ease.

Precision and precedent are the hallmarks of *Britannia*. As a result the ship's company are unlike any on the high seas. She is an independent command, administered personally by the Flag Officer Royal Yachts, the only Admiral to

Above left: Flower show. The Queen Mother and Princess Margaret, bouquets in hand, arrive on shore.

Right: Hop, skip and jump. The Queen leaps ashore (above) with a helping hand from the Turkish Prime Minister during a visit to the country in 1971. And (below) Prince Charles provides assistance for Princess Diana during a landing on their Canadian tour. A recce party from the yacht always goes ahead to ensure that there are no royal slip-ups caused by steep slopes or greasy quay steps.

be a Captain at the same time. He is normally appointed as an extra equerry to the Queen and as such is a member of the Royal Household. When the Queen is on board he has a very close working relationship with her, and every day he discusses with her details of the route and day-to-day events on board. 'The Queen, Prince Philip and Prince Charles all take a very keen interest in where we are going and what is going on,' says Rear Admiral Greening.

The yacht's company numbers twenty-one officers and 256 men. Officers are appointed for a two-year stretch of duty, as are half the ratings. The other half are permanent members and stay with the yacht for their navy career. It goes without saying that all are hand-picked, meeting the highest standards of seamanship and behaviour. The feeling among the ship's company is like that of working for an old-established family firm. Loyalties are strong and affection mutual. When a rating leaves after completing ten years' service he will always go for a chat with the Queen when she is on board to say goodbye. Many Yachtsmen she knows by name. 'When a chap leaves the Queen's sentiment is, "There goes a man who has served the family business well",' said one officer.

Fourteen officers and 159 men are engaged in navigation, watchkeeping, communications, engine-room and electrical duties, while five officers and 54 men carry out the functions of supply and secretariat, medical and shipwright duties. All are volunteers, and are known as 'Yachtsmen', or 'Snotty Yachties' by other, more envious crews. They receive no special benefits in terms of pay

'One of the most important things about our job is to ensure that when the Queen is on board she can relax in pleasant and peaceful surroundings.'

BRITANNIA'S CAPTAIN,
REAR ADMIRAL PAUL GREENING

Opposite, top left: The Queen and Prince Philip are piped on board before setting out on their 1972 Silver Wedding cruise.

Opposite, top right: A yachtsman shins up a rope ladder from the royal barge.

Opposite, below: The ship's company raise the dress flags. They pride themselves on being able to carry out this feat in three seconds. Visitors always ask what the symbols on these multicoloured flags mean. The answer is quite simple: nothing; they are just for show.

allowances or leave. Traditions of dress on board include the wearing of a special No. 1 naval uniform with serge jumpers tucked inside the top of the trousers and finished at the back with a black silk bow, introduced by Queen Victoria as a symbol of mourning for her husband, Prince Albert. On all blue uniforms ratings wear white badges instead of the red which are customary in the general service. With the royal yacht flash on the right arm and a cap ribbon with a crown between the words 'Royal' and 'Yacht', a *Britannia* uniform is the most distinctive in the Navy.

Officers, however, wear exactly the same uniform as the rest of the Navy except that they don't wear a link button in their mess jackets. This dates to the time King Edward VII's valet made a mistake in his master's dress when he dined in the officers' wardroom. Naturally those present adjusted their dress to conform, and so the custom was born. In the royal apartments, abaft the mainmast, the men go hatless because this puts them technically out of uniform, thus sparing the Queen the bother of returning salutes when she is on deck taking the air.

Procedures and customs

But the most striking feature of life on board is the quiet. If the Navy were a monastic service, the royal yacht would be a silent order. Every year the men are issued with a pair of starched white rubber-soled plimsolls so as not to mark the spotless teak decks or disturb the royals. As far as possible orders are carried out without spoken word or command. A shouted order or a raised voice would be unthinkable. *Britannia* has an alarm bell, of course, but that is used for real emergencies such as fire. From berthing to casting off everything is conducted with the minimum of fuss and noise.

Urgent instructions such as an altered time of sailing are passed on by means of special noticeboards around the accommodation quarters. A 'hot' notice means urgent action, a 'red hot' message means it should have been done five minutes ago. However, no one moves at the double, always at the quick. The ratings are the only ones in the Navy to be called by their Christian names.

Other methods of passing orders are by flag, semaphore or walkie-talkie. For example, 'Out ladders and boom' is signalled from the bridge by flag. For anchoring or securing to buoys, boat work or handling ropes and wires, the officer in charge carries a small wooden bat. By moving a hinged flap he shows a coloured disc. Green means 'hoist', yellow, 'lower' and red, 'stop'.

It is fitting therefore that the élite of the Fleet have a number of ancient customs and traditions which set *Britannia* apart from every other ship in the world. On other warships, 'piping the side' is an honour accorded to all commanding officers and several other senior ranks, but on *Britannia* the Queen alone is so honoured. She can make exceptions, though, for foreign heads of state or foreign sovereigns in naval uniform, and she broke with tradition during her six-day visit to America in 1976, when she gave permission for former President Gerald Ford to be piped on board for a farewell banquet, and similarly for President Reagan and his wife during her Californian tour in 1983. The Queen explained that this was 'to highlight the respect for the position of the President of the United States by the United Kingdom.'

Piping the side is an ancient custom dating from the days of sailing ships when the captain was hoisted in and out of the ship in a boatswain's chair to the tune of the boatswain's whistle, which was used to call attention or give an order. It is carried out by the boatswain or his mate and the piping consists of a long whistle of about twelve seconds, beginning on a low note, rising to medium and falling to a low note again.

On board *Britannia* the tradition of drinking the health of the sovereign

Left and above: The timeless quality of naval reviews is captured in these two pictures, virtually identical but with more than forty years between them. Cheered by the men of HMS London, *the* Victoria and Albert III *sails grandly by during the Spithead Review of 1937 (left) and* Britannia *reviews the fleet in 1977 (above), with sailors from the aircraft carrier* Ark Royal *cheering the Queen in precise naval fashion.*

sitting down – due to low ceilings – is broken. On the royal yacht the toast is always drunk standing as an extra mark of respect. At noon on the Queen's birthday, all officers meet in the wardroom to drink her health.

Within such a select band, the *esprit de corps* is high and, as befits the First Lady of the Royal Navy, the standards of seamanship the slickest and most flamboyant. And where ceremony and seamanship combine, *Britannia* reigns supreme. At the Silver Jubilee Naval Review at Spithead in 1977 she was superb. 'One of the most romantic, moving sights I have ever seen in my life,' said one observer after watching the royal yacht sailing slowly down the ranks of 157 warships, 97 of them British. Along the fifteen-mile line-up, 30,000 sailors stepped smartly one pace forward to salute the Queen as she passed by. Every man on deck held the guard rail either side of him, as though linking arms with his neighbour. At the carefully rehearsed command, off came all the caps, to be held at arm's length and rotated once clockwise with every cheer, just as the drill book prescribes. Their cheering floated down the wind – 'Hurray' and not 'Hurrah' as at previous naval reviews, by the Queen's request. There was a brief show of the royal yacht's flag handling as the Royal Standard, Admiralty Flag and Union Flag were hauled down and simultaneously replaced for the return leg of the sail past.

Ratings pride themselves on being able to raise the forty-six multicoloure
dress flags in three seconds. Wherever possible the captain will spurn th
approaches of tugs when docking. When she berthed in Sydney in 195
Britannia set an all-time record for speed in approach and tying up – fou
minutes to be precise. Under the command of Vice Admiral Sir Connoll
Abel Smith, the royal yacht raked past the cruiser Newcastle with only a foo
clearance. As she thundered down on the wharf, the watching crow
scattered, fearing a collision. The manoeuvre was variously described as
'sailor's dream', a 'miracle of seamanship' or simply 'plain stupid'.

Rear Admiral Greening says, 'We don't use tugs unless there's a stron
wind, although we always have them standing by. The yacht is a wonderf
emblem for Britain and the more competently and efficiently we handle th
boat the better the image we produce for Britain. When the Queen is on boar
everything has to be spot on and it detracts from the occasion to have a coup
of tugs tow you in.'

Such skills become merely routine on a sophisticated showboat lik
Britannia. As a matter of day-to-day calculation, the navigator may have t
take into account the number of native canoes, bum boats, pleasure craf
punts, rafts and even bathtubs Britannia may encounter on her regal progress t
shore. During one visit to Vancouver, where an annual bathtub race
customary, she was met by a flotilla of these homely craft. This kind of routin
razzmatazz means that she gets into a fair share of scrapes.

Like the floating show-woman she is, Britannia never raises a porthole
some of the more exotic gifts that crowd into her hold. During a tour of th
Seychelles the Queen was given a giant tortoise, in The Gambia a bab
crocodile came her way gift-wrapped in a pierced silver biscuit tin. It du
ended up in the bath of her private secretary, Sir Martin Charteris. In Fi
natives brought an enormous roast pig on board. An admirer in Brazil placed

*Above: Hats off to the Queen as
Britannia steams past Three Rivers in
the heart of Canada, during the
inaugural journey down the St Lawrence
Seaway in 1959.*

sloth on board *Britannia* while she was docked at Recife. It lay lazily on deck in a box for several hours and refused to budge in spite of the best efforts of the cooing crewmen. It went eventually, box and all.

As a rule animals are not allowed on board, but during the Princess of Wales' Canadian tour ratings befriended a stray racing pigeon called Percy. It ended up in Ontario, and its owner, 4000 miles away in Cheshire, England, thought he had a world-record-breaker on his hands. Although this feathered stowaway was no superbird, it did receive VIP treatment from the company, dining on beer and biscuits in its own cage. 'At first it was a real pest, but the boys grew very fond of him,' said one rating.

It is little wonder the stowaway pigeon had to stay on deck: space below is confined. Before a major refit in 1972 the company's quarters would have been recognized by Lord Nelson. Hammocks slung across passageways, bunk beds in corridors or in the tropics on the open deck. In one mess just 30-ft (9-m) long, 12-ft (3.6-m) wide and tapering to 4-ft (1.2-m) at one end, 18 men slept. After the improvements in 1972 one rating commented, 'You don't get your feet in your breakfast anymore.'

Space has always been a problem on royal yachts. In 1881 the Admiralty gave permission for men to take their service rations on shore because there just wasn't enough room to move on board. The first *Victoria and Albert* attracted criticism from one politician who complained, 'The royal apartments are luxurious but the ship's company was crammed into wretched dog holes with not enough room to move.'

These days every man has a bunk and locker, and there are large recreation and canteen facilities. Homely touches are added by the men, and in the petty officers' mess plaques bearing the coat of arms or crest of their home towns decorate the walls.

But reminders of the 'old firm' are never far away. In the officers' dining

Above: With views like this to look forward to, this time in Fiji, it's little wonder that the yacht's crew boast that a berth on Britannia is the most glamorous in the Navy.

Above: The Queen and Prince Philip accept the salute from their escort ship during a tour of the Bahamas in 1975.

Right: One of the ceremonial Royal Marines guards Britannia's gangway. Security is tight on the royal yacht. Although no guns are carried, officers boast that it is as 'safe as a battleship'.

room the walls have a series of signed pictures of members of the royal family that the average photographic agency would kill for. Their silver cutlery and cruets are all from the *Victoria and Albert*, even their napkin rings, kept in orderly pigeon holes, are from the old royal yacht.

Loyalty to the monarch is total, and the dedication of officers and crew is unquestionable. As one rating said, 'It's a tough job but the best in the Navy.' Their sense of tradition, too, is every bit as strong as the royal family's. Every Christmas for sixty years the children's ward of the Queen Alexandra's Hospital, near Portsmouth, has come to expect a specially baked and decorated cake from the company. While the royals are on duty on tour, the men regularly take on local rugby, cricket and soccer teams. Several of the present *Britannia* company would make good non-League soccer players. During Cowes week the crew muster useful yacht and water polo teams, and the twelve-oar cutters used to regularly take part in competitions.

A popular cricket fixture is that played between a *Britannia* side and King Edward's school at Witley. The prize is a ladies' glove – the same glove, unclaimed, that was found after a match in 1923. Every year the officers and their wives receive invitations to Ascot and a Buckingham Palace garden party. The ratings always get their chance for a chat with the 'family firm' when the royals visit their messes at the end of every cruise. Long-serving crew members are eligible to receive the Queen's personal award, the Royal Victorian medal – further evidence of the close links between the royals and the yacht. Indeed, before any tour programme is decided, the Queen always checks to make sure that 'her boys' don't have to cancel leave to fit in with her plans. As Prince Philip says of the ship's company: 'They become trusted friends and they care for the yacht with a quiet and proud efficiency.'

Above right: Security screen. Motorcycle outriders and ceremonial guards on horseback (top) ensure the Queen's safety as she leaves Britannia during a visit to Tunisia in 1980. In 1983, as Britannia makes her majestic entrance into San Diego harbour (bottom), American Navy guards circle the yacht in a high-speed rubber dinghy. The rule for welcoming boats is to keep 300 yards (275 metres) away from them.

With such close ties to the royal family it is not surprising that *Britannia* is the one Royal Navy ship without a policeman. As Able Seaman Ken Douglas commented: 'The attraction of working on the royal yacht is that you discipline yourself. You don't have somebody breathing down your neck all the time.' There are no fines to be imposed, but no second chances either. Bringing girls on board, wild drunken nights, fighting ashore are all offences that will get a rating sent back to general service. If the offence is serious enough and the yacht is away from Portsmouth the rating can even be flown back home. Such problems are few and far between, although the ship was deeply shaken when a homosexual vice ring was uncovered on board. It led to nine Yachtsmen serving jail sentences.

While they are restrained on board, if you meet the ratings on shore they

will be eager to prove how red-blooded they are. From San Diego to Sydney they find that all the nice girls love a sailor – especially if he's wearing a royal yacht uniform. They rarely go on the town in civilian clothes, preferring to wear their 'No. 1 Fishing Gear' – those distinctive yacht uniforms – in the hope of catching a pretty girl. As one 'Yachtie' boasted, 'Royal yacht sailors have girls dying to go out with them in every port. It's the most glamorous posting in the Navy.' Adelaide, Australia seems to be favourite. Twice men from *Britannia* have met girls of their dreams there and married.

One squad on board whose members rarely have time to enjoy life ashore are the nine Royal Marines, who act as ceremonial guards. When *Britannia* is berthed they man the royal gangways, resplendent in their smart uniforms. A Marine acts as the yacht's butcher, a corporal as the postman for every man on board, while the other seven men give a round-the-clock orderly service for the royals on board. 'A kind of super-efficient hotel porter,' says one officer.

Their work in no way supplements the role of the Scotland Yard detectives who always travel with the royal family even on board the yacht, but three Royal Marine crewmen act as divers, daily swimming under the hull to check for terrorist devices such as limpet mines or snags in the propellor.

Security is taken seriously, although as one former captain said, '*Britannia* carries no weapons, but she is safe as a battleship.' Just as well, given the number of VIPs who spend time on board. The Beat Retreat ceremony with President and Mrs Reagan was delayed for ten minutes when divers spotted bubbles rising from near the yacht in San Francisco harbour. The all clear was given after further checks, but during the Queen's visit to Ulster in 1977 the possibility of an attack on the yacht by the Irish Republican Army was seriously considered. One senior British official was quoted as saying, 'An attack on *Britannia* might sound fantastic, but could become real.'

The ring of steel surrounding the royals was allegedly breached during a visit to Portugal. As part of the visit the Queen called on a Lisbon seminary which used to be a British naval base during the Napoleonic Wars. The story goes that the seminary was entitled to fly the White Ensign and also to demand a new one from visiting ships. When the Queen called she offered the rector a new flag from *Britannia* to maintain the tradition, but the rector replied politely, 'We already have it.' It seems that enthusiastic students had staged a night raid on the yacht, sneaking its White Ensign and leaving the seminary's old one in its place!

The royal yacht is always accompanied by an escort destroyer, for diplomatic and security purposes. During one tour, *Britannia*, her escort and a refuelling vessel were crossing the Indian Ocean when the oiler developed engine trouble. The escort had to leave the yacht to help the refuelling ship back to port. *Britannia* found herself alone, miles away from the nearest land.

Soon afterwards, the officers on watch spotted a Russian warship on the horizon. This was no chance encounter; for a whole day the Soviet destroyer shadowed the royal yacht, the Queen and Prince Philip watching her from their quarters. Without arms or assistance nearby, *Britannia* was a vulnerable target. The Queen remained calm if edgy throughout this cat-and-mouse game. She later told friends: 'It was a very creepy feeling. I never felt any real sense of menace. It just made one feel very uneasy to know that we were in the middle of the ocean being tailed by a Russian ship.'

But such events do not occur often; the safety, comfort and privacy of the Queen and other members of the royal family is always the number one priority for the ship's company. And when the call comes their first consideration is always to get the royal show back in business. Wherever they might be in the world it is these uniformed scene shifters who always ensure that the royals put on a command performance and that *Britannia* is the one theatre where everyone comes away smiling.

Above: A lone yachtsman serenades his friends during an evening's relaxation on the forecastle. During a voyage there may be several organized concerts on board. The Queen loves to attend these good-humoured affairs. As one royal aide says: 'You find burly yachtsmen dressed in white ankle socks and gymslips prancing around on stage. It's great fun and because the Royal Marine band is so professional it gives the most amateur production a touch of class.'

5

FLYING THE FLAG

'The dramatic effect of the Royal Yacht leaving port with thousands of cheering people watching the Queen go is enormous.'

SIR RUPERT NEVILL, FORMER PRIVATE
SECRETARY TO PRINCE PHILIP

Most of us, when we go overseas, take a couple of suitcases, tuck our passports into our pockets, and make our way to the airport. The Queen is different. For a start she doesn't need a passport. As they are all issued in her name, there's not much point. But she does take with her between two and five tons of luggage. When the Queen flies the flag for Britain a small army travels with her to ensure there is nothing half mast about the affair. It is an army organized with military precision.

Everything from the tasteful cufflink presents for Embassy officials to the famous bottles of Malvern water for the Queen's tea is carefully labelled, stowed and packed into blue trunks whose outsides are distinguished by the marking 'The Queen' embossed in gold or white letters. They are carried on board *Britannia* by ratings and stowed in the hold. The royal baggage can

'February and March are usually good times for foreign visits. There's not much going on here and in any case the weather's usually better abroad.'

PRINCE PHILIP

Above: One of the Queen's trunks stands on the quayside before being loaded. When the Queen and Prince Philip go on a state visit, they may take as much as five tons of luggage with them.

Previous page: A typical South Seas idyll. Britannia sometimes seems to cast a spell over people: one tribe made Prince Philip a god after they watched Britannia sail by.

include everything that is portable: strawberry jam, Dundee cake, polo sticks, Kendal mint cake, a wreath of poppies, autographed royal pictures in silver frames, hot-water bottles, copies of Prince Philip's latest book (for gifts), a feather pillow, the Queen's electric kettle and, if Prince Charles is on board, extra rations of honey and sausages – plus his own windsurfer, of course.

Royal tours on board *Britannia* always have a practical, diplomatic purpose. She doesn't swan around the world's seaways burning fuel oil at a rate of seven miles to the ton just to keep the crew out of mischief. As the Queen's official residence abroad, the royal yacht has a dual role when the royal family go visiting – flying the flag for Britain's exports and consolidating links with Commonwealth countries. For example, *Britannia* has gone where no plane could have landed: to the islands of Tristan da Cunha and St Helena, and to sundry smudges of red in the South Pacific.

Britannia has helped the Queen become the most travelled monarch the world has ever known. In addition to helping her fulfil her role as head of the Commonwealth, the royal yacht is central in planning the elaborate and sophisticated public relations exercises on behalf of Britain.

For example, when the Queen and Prince Philip flew to Kuwait on Concorde, they used *Britannia* as a floating hotel while they visited British engineering projects in the oil-rich Arab nations. When the Queen goes out to bat for Britain, she has the prestige of the monarchy behind her, which no political office can ever match. And *Britannia* plays a fine back-up role. She is not used simply to convey the royal family from state to state, but as a salt-water palace, and like a palace, she has many functions: entertaining VIPs; hosting high-powered meetings between businessmen or heads of state; accommodating investitures, receptions and banquets. The Queen does not have to rely on hotel rooms or Embassy residences to do her entertaining. She can be a hostess in her own home, at ease in familiar surroundings.

Royal tours are usually suggested first by the Foreign Office in response to an invitation. Meetings at Buckingham Palace flesh out the bare bones of the idea and further weight is added after royal aides visit the host country to reconnoitre and to pencil in the fine detail. The usual procedure is for *Britannia* to steam on ahead of the royals, leaving Portsmouth several weeks before the Queen flies out. As soon as the Queen and the Household touch down, her dresser and maid promptly drive to the royal yacht to lay out and press her dresses, prepare her bedroom and set out the mirrors, combs and brushes in readiness for the arrival of Her Majesty. Petty Officer Ian Maudsley will have been busy preparing and arranging flowers for the royal rooms, and a dozen other little touches will have been made to give the Queen's rooms that 'home from home' feeling. And once the Queen has been piped aboard the yacht moves up into full 'touring gear'.

At every new country on the tour, the travelling and home press corps are invited on board for a reception lasting anything from between thirty minutes to an hour. It's a chance for the royal family to strike a few blows at one of their perennial sparring partners, the press, and for the press to hit back with some questions they would not normally get in the ring with.

For the most part these receptions are good-natured affairs with little blood spilt on either side. Stiff white and gold invitation cards are given out beforehand, and those lucky enough to receive one arrive at the red-carpeted gangway of *Britannia* to be met by courteous naval officers. Bags and coats are left behind and, after a quick look in a mirror lashed to a beam, you climb the wooden stairs to the shelter deck, covered by a buff-coloured awning. A little nervously you stand in line, waiting for your name and organization to be read out as an introduction. The Queen and Prince Philip are there to greet you. You bow slightly, shake hands, then move on, the official welcome over. You

Above: *The Queen wearing a jaunty nautical cap that had commentators recalling Carnaby Street fashions of the 1960s. She wore the cap for her review of a guard of honour when she disembarked at San Diego in February 1983.*

Left: *The Queen and the diminutive Sheik of Bahrain stand for their national anthems. With temperatures of more than 30°C (86°F), the colourful canopy is not simply for show.*

go in search of *Britannia's* famed hospitality, and are relieved to find a steward carrying a silver tray laden with generous drinks.

Royal protocol has often confused foreign dignitaries. Many men – including a baffled bishop in New Zealand – have followed their wife's example, and curtsied before the Queen!

At these press receptions, the rule is never to divulge the contents of a conversation. It is a rule which is often broken, but the revelations are innocent enough. In San Diego, it was reported that the Queen was asked if she preferred being a monarch to a pauper. Naturally she replied that she preferred being monarch. On one occasion in Chicago Prince Philip was asked about the colour of his underpants! (he didn't know) and, during her Canada tour, the Princess of Wales revealed to a local woman journalist that she didn't like to see the nasty things written about her plastered all over the front pages. Sure enough, her confidential comments were duly banner-headlined in that journal. At one reception a photographer, to his eternal embarrassment, accidently spilled drink over the Queen, forcing her to go and change her dress. But for the most part, receptions are well-behaved affairs, guests gossiping for days afterwards about their impressions.

The press side-show over, the tour routine can get underway. Usually the Queen disembarks at 10a.m. sharp, either by the starboard-after stairway to the royal barge or down the red-carpeted gangway. Following her day's duties on shore, she is back on board by 6p.m., discussing tour details with her private secretary or press officer before having a quiet hour to herself in preparation for that evening's banquet.

Planning and protocol

Dinners on the royal yacht are very special occasions; events which have been planned right down to the printed menu long before *Britannia* leaves England. When the royal family are on board, the Buckingham Palace chef takes control of the kitchens. He brings with him three other chefs – one in charge of pastry – and a kitchen porter. As might be expected, the royal galley is palatial. Mrs Beaton herself would have admired the gleaming ranks of copper pans, some of which have been in service since 1866, many bearing the inscription of the previous royal yacht. The two Admiralty ovens can cope with a hundred chickens (enough to feed 440 men if it were ever converted into a hospital ship). There is a huge four-tier steamer for puddings which can cater for 200; a cold room big enough to keep two months' supply of meat and fish, and a dairy and vegetable room with space to feed the whole ship for a month. Fresh bread is made daily, and where possible, local vegetables are bought to supplement supplies.

The wines for the meal are chosen in London and stored in the wine cellar. As one officer joked, 'Wine must travel well on the yacht.' As in other ships, the wine racks are caged in and bolted to the floor to stop undue movement in a storm. Where possible the Queen likes to choose local vintages, as a compliment to the country visited – even though they're bought in England. For the thirty-first wedding anniversary banquet for President and Mrs Reagan on board *Britannia* – which was docked in Pier 50, San Francisco – the wines were Californian, although the champagne, Bollinger '75, was French.

As the guests, the cream of Californian society, arrived at the quayside, a large crowd watched their shiny limousines spilling out their contents of furs, medals, and black ties. When they walked on board, they were photographed by 'Snaps', the yacht's cameraman, who quickly processed the photos in the ship's darkroom so that guests could be presented with a framed souvenir picture as they left.

They were escorted to the drawing room where the royal and presidential

Opposite: Light show. Britannia *is lit up by a brilliant display of fireworks during a visit to the West Indies in 1966.*

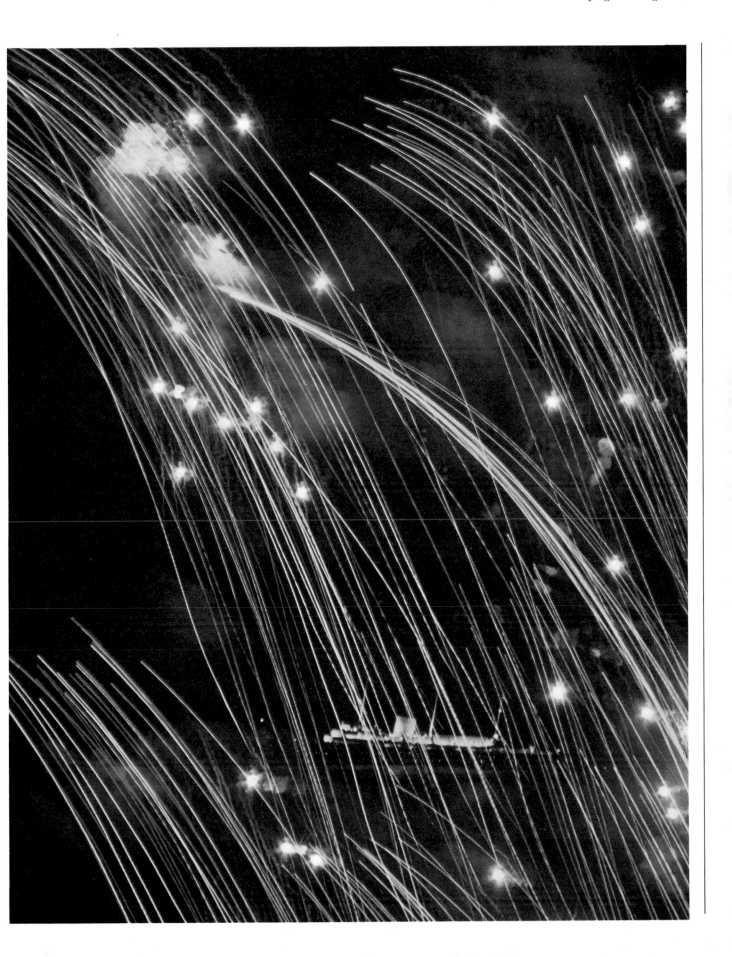

Above: Anniversary celebration. Ronald and Nancy Reagan pose for pictures with the Queen and the Duke of Edinburgh before a dinner in San Francisco held to celebrate the Reagans' thirty-first wedding anniversary. President Reagan drank only orange juice, leaving his glass on the baby grand piano.

couples were standing in a receiving line. Aperitifs were served, members of the Household and yacht officers in full dress uniform joining in the small-talk. At one banquet during the Queen's visit to Morocco in 1980, a Lady in Waiting asked the eldest prince of King Hassan if he liked the sea. The child, just ten, and dressed in a miniature dinner-jacket, puffed out his chest and said, 'I am Commander of the Fleet'.

At a given signal, the centre doors dividing the dining room off are opened and the guests, a gentleman taking each lady's arm, parade through. The Reagans and the Queen and Prince Philip stayed behind for a moment for official photographs, the President carefully placing his orange-juice on the grand piano.

The dining table itself is a work of art, and for a banquet it takes three hours to set. The position of every knife, fork, spoon and glass is measured by ruler before the Keeper of the Royal Apartments, Lieutenant Commander Nick Carter, is satisfied that everything is perfectly in place. Napkins artistically folded sit alongside the programme of music and the menu – always in French and given at the end of the meal as a souvenir. The occasional guest has been known to take one of the silver napkin holders as a memento. 'We have to take them aside and ask them to give up their trophies,' said one officer.

Each place setting has five Brierley crystal glasses, each engraved with the Queen's cypher; one for water, two for wine, one for champagne, the other for port. The crockery is white Minton china, again with the royal cypher and gold trim, while for dessert and coffee, a green and gold Spode Copeland service is brought out from the special pantry in the kitchens.

The centre displays on the mahogany table are priceless. Favourites of the Queen are the 150-year-old solid silver Nelson and Collingwood trophies presented after the Battle of Trafalgar. A statue given by the Sultan of Oman is a more recent table decoration. It is an 18-in (46-cm) high carving of a humble camel with a calf under two palm-trees. But it's in solid gold and every tiny detail is exquisitely wrought. At the right of the Queen's place, at the top of the table, is placed a handy silver notepad with an etching of *Britannia* on the cover.

At the Reagans' banquet, white-jacketed stewards and royal staff resplendent in full dress attended to the needs of the fifty-six diners, while in the adjoining room a section of the Royal Marine band played a selection of tunes from *Oklahoma* and *Showboat*. As a grand finale, there was a specially composed anniversary waltz for the Reagans. 'When I married Nancy I promised her many things, but never this,' said a delighted President at the end of the evening.

As the perfect hostess, the Queen must always be conscious of the evening's timetable, and normally by 9.30 dinner is over and the guests retire to an anteroom to enjoy cigars and brandy. This gives Nick Carter and his skilled scene-shifters enough time to clear the covers, dismantle the tables, vacuum the carpet and rig the bars. As one officer commented, 'It's an incredible operation, like a well-oiled machine going into action.' For on this night the dinner guests were joined by another 200 VIPs to watch Beat Retreat from the deck of *Britannia*. This stunning ceremony of military music and precision marching takes place on the quayside. It starts under floodlight at 10.45p.m., and nothing stops the progress of these marching men. During her trip to Morocco, the King's guards were standing on the quayside just before the band were due to march. Undeterred, the band played on, the guards scattering.

During a trip to Germany, the Queen, as is customary, lined the rails with the other guests to watch the floodlit proceedings, and after the fifteen-minute display, the guest conductor was invited on board. The message was duly delivered, the German conductor looked up at the Queen beckoning to him from above and hastened to board, but unfortunately, he chose the crew's gangway – about 150 yards (137 m) from the Queen – to make his entrance. The confused conductor floundered about, lost in the company's quarters, and never did get to meet Her Majesty.

As a special treat for the Reagans, the Queen organized a late-night party for thirty guests. They were given an iced fruit-cake with a single candle on top by the Queen and the crew presented them with a greetings card showing a cartoon of the President trying to pull his horse on board the ship. The President's deputy chief of staff, Michael Deaver, lifted the lid of the baby grand and played 'True Love'. Nobody minded the fact that for most of the night, the President's standard was flying upside down on *Britannia*'s mast.

Storms at sea

The anniversary banquet was the highlight of the Queen's California tour in 1983. But *Britannia* nearly didn't make it. She had to battle through 25-ft (7.6-m) seas and a full-blown gale. It took her 42 hours to cover the 368 miles (590-km) from Long Beach to San Francisco. Nancy Reagan was supposed to travel with the Queen up the Californian coast, passing under Golden Gate Bridge, but in the end the Queen watched from the President's plane, circling overhead, as *Britannia* made her grand entrance. In fact storms turned the carefully prepared schedule upside down. During her visit, the Queen suffered tempests, tornadoes and floods; indeed the only thing missing was a biblical plague of frogs!

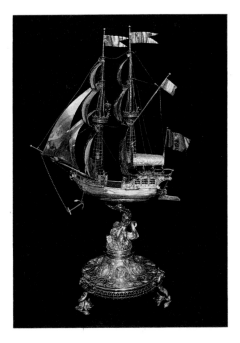

Top: Now part of the dining-room decorations, this silver-gilt sailing ship, originally used as a wine cooler, was made in France in the sixteenth century.

Above: Also in the dining room is the Nelson Vase, presented on behalf of the nation to Viscountess Nelson 'as a lasting memorial of the transcendent and heroic achievements of the ever-to-be lamented warrior Horatio Nelson'.

Above: Night moves. The Queen watches the Royal Marine band Beat Retreat. This evening spectacle draws huge crowds to watch the breathtaking display of precision marching and musicianship.

The Queen's childhood dream of visiting Hollywood and California turned into an incredible, real-life Wild West adventure that proved to be one of the most memorable state visits of her reign. It left her with memories of a stomach-churning ride in a four-wheel-drive truck to the Reagan's ranch through flooded roads, of impromptu visits to local restaurants, and of sitting round the campfire at the President's ranch swapping yarns. At the height of the storms which ripped through the state, the Queen was on board *Britannia* as she heaved and strained at her moorings in Pier 9, Long Beach. She later told friends, 'It was one of the most terrifying nights of my life.'

In the royal suite she could hear the 1½-in (1.3-cm) thick steel hawsers snapping as the swell rose and fell. By morning the roads were under four feet of water and the Queen had to abandon her black bullet-proof limousine for a battered grey Navy bus. She walked off *Britannia* in black wellingtons and, under the protection of a brolly, clambered aboard for a crazy charabanc ride. The frenzied arrangements to obtain the bus caused amusement at the expense of one *Britannia* officer. This officer was shouting down the ship-to-shore telephone link, trying to convince his American Navy counterpart that the Queen would be prepared to travel by bus. When the American demurred, the conversation became heated. Choice examples of Anglo-Saxon were exchanged but the *Britannia* officer made his point. Triumphantly he put down the phone and then, to his horror, realized the Queen had been listening. Blushing, he tried to stammer out an apology. But she smiled sweetly and said, 'I've been married to a sailor for thirty-six years and I've heard it all before.'

Bad weather and *Britannia* are old opponents, and over the years the Queen has learnt to cope with a bumpy sea journey. The myth is that the Queen is a bad sailor and for this reason does not like to travel on the royal yacht. The truth is that the Queen adores *Britannia* and, in the words of one officer, 'is no worse and no better than anyone else as far as seasickness is concerned.' She takes her own medication during a rough crossing. As one royal doctor said, 'She faces this sort of thing. She doesn't like heavy weather but she knows what to do.'

Her trips to America seem to be fated to attract the Furies. As *Britannia* battled through a force nine gale to visit New York in 1977, the Queen seemed

Above right: An American Air Force colonel shelters the Queen with an umbrella as she makes her way to her plane to Santa Barbara and President Reagan's ranch. A battered Navy bus had had to drive her from Long Beach Naval base to the airport through four feet (1.2 metres) of floodwater.

'almost merry' as she appeared for a drink before dinner. According to Susan Crosland, Prince Philip looked 'ashen and drawn'. Dinner was quickly over, and as the ship lurched from side to side like a giddy pendulum, the Queen attempted to open the sliding doors. Susan Crosland continues the story: 'The Queen gripped the handle firmly, pressed her back to the door and moved with it as it slid slowly shut. "Wheeeeeee", said the Queen. *Britannia* shuddered and reeled. "Wheeeeeee", said the Queen again. She managed to slip through the doors with a quick "Goodnight" before the next lurch.

'The next day every one was feeling rather better. "I have never seen so many grey and grim faces round a dinner table," said the Queen. She paused. "Philip was not at all well." She paused. "I'm glad to say." She giggled. I'd forgotten that her Consort is an Admiral of the Fleet!'

Above: The Queen and Prince Philip arrive by rubber dinghy at Ship Cove near Picton on South Island in New Zealand, where Captain Cook landed in 1770.

On that occasion, the welcome in New York was worth it; hundreds of boats hooting as *Britannia* sailed by the Statue of Liberty framed against the Manhattan skyline.

During another storm on a tour of New Zealand in 1970, the Queen was woken in her cabin to be told that three men from *Britannia*'s escorting frigate had been washed overboard and that the royal yacht's first lieutenant was trapped in her forecastle. The Duke of Edinburgh was on the bridge watching helplessly as 40-ft (12-m) waves crashed over the officer. His only link with the bridge was a two-way radio, over which Prince Philip and other officers encouraged him to cling on. After twenty minutes, battered and bruised, he was able to dash to safety.

The southerly gale in the notorious Cook Strait was blowing at 60 knots and watchers ashore saw *Britannia* disappear time and again in the troughs. Aboard the yacht, glasses and unsecured furniture flew, including a television set which got such a thump that it turned itself on. Of the three men overboard, two were saved; the other lost. *Britannia* could not help in the rescue operation because, as one royal aide said, 'She was at emergency stations herself'. The yacht, pitching heavily, ploughed into the storm and tidal rips where the Tasman Sea meets the Pacific Ocean at a mere four knots and found it difficult to turn into the entrance to Tory Channel, her planned route to Picton. When they finally entered Picton Harbour for the Bicentenary celebrations, the Queen donned a pair of slacks and a fawn wind-cheater, tied a scarf round her head and jumped ashore from a rubber dinghy in the cove where Captain Cook landed 200 years previously. From chairs on the beach, she and Prince Philip watched a lively re-enactment of the original landing, with war-painted Maoris whooping it up and Cook's men offering beads as currency. Once again *Britannia* had made it, and the crowds who had waited in eager anticipation were not disappointed.

Commonwealth tours

Years earlier, on these same seas, she had proved her worth in one of the most testing voyages of her career. In 1956, Prince Philip had the idea of using the royal yacht to visit all those off-the-beaten-track islands owing allegiance to Britain. The aim was to pull closer the gossamer threads of the new Queen's Commonwealth, to shine a light in the dark corners of Empire.

It was a glorious adventure which meant sacrificing four months with his family. Indeed, when he broadcast to the Commonwealth at Christmas, from his study on board *Britannia*, his voice was eagerly listened to by the Queen, Prince Charles and Princess Anne at the royal retreat of Sandringham. In her own broadcast, millions heard her say, 'You will understand me when I tell you that of all the voices we have heard this afternoon, none has given my children and myself greater joy than that of my husband.'

During his four-month leave of absence, Philip ranged from the rain forests of Papua New Guinea to the icy wastes of the Antarctic.

On board *Britannia*, he learned to paint under the guidance of Edward Seago, played deck hockey with vigour, and even had a go at a game of tennis on an ice-floe. 'Rather inexpert,' he recalled. In Papua New Guinea, he was dubbed by natives, 'The man who belong Missus Queen.' In future times, the Prince's presence was to have a rather strange effect on these South Sea islanders. When *Britannia* sailed close by the New Hebrides in 1974, the natives decided that Prince Philip was the Messiah who would return to work miracles, curing all sickness and making the old young again. The 200 villagers, members of the Iounhanan tribe, even sent him a gift of a 5-ft (1.5-m) long pig-sticking implement. In return, and perhaps in order to stave off trouble on the island, the Duke sent an autographed picture of himself. They are still awaiting his return in the royal yacht.

Below: The heads of the Commonwealth join the Queen on the veranda deck of Britannia *for a formal photograph.*

Above: A bearded Prince Philip views the simple cross in memory of the Antarctic explorer Sir Ernest Shackleton which overlooks Grytviken in South Georgia.

*Opposite: Images of Canada.
Prince Charles and Prince Edward (top left) at the 1976 Montreal Olympics. At first the Queen felt that Edward was too young to go, but he was so eager to see big sister Anne compete in the Games' riding events that the Queen relented.
A Mountie looks on (top right) as the royal yacht approaches Charlottetown during the 1983 tour of Canada with the Prince and Princess of Wales.
Prince Andrew (below) waves to the crowds from the deck of Britannia. He stayed for two terms at Lakefield College in 1976.*

During that 1957 adventure, he didn't get around to pig-sticking, but he did watch whales being harpooned, and visited a whaling station at Grytviken in South Georgia. 'The stench made strong men quail,' one observer recalls. Here too he viewed the simple cross left in memory of the courageous explorer Sir Ernest Shackleton, who died during an expedition to the Antarctic.

As the royal yacht picked her way through the ice-studded South Atlantic, the Prince organized a beard-growing contest – 116 followed his example – and he designed the 'Red Nose' certificates for the ship's company after they entered the Antarctic Circle. At an ice-bound survey base at Deception Island, he showed a film – *Seven Brides for Seven Brothers* – for the lonely scientists. He later confessed, 'I'm not sure whether it was a good idea or whether it was perhaps slightly misjudged.'

Three years later, during a second solo Commonwealth tour on *Britannia* – this time to the Pacific Islands – he faced a similar ticklish problem when two Buckingham Palace secretaries were given hoola-hoops. The bikini-clad pair insisted on practising the art on deck as the sun was setting. The crew, who had had no shore leave for seven weeks, watched them through binoculars, until one day they sent in a protest complaining that the girls were trying their self-restraint. They were tactfully asked to stop their gyrations.

Christmas Day spent on *Britannia*, as the Prince spent it during that '57 voyage, has its own rituals. The Prince judged the decorations of the various messes, and just for the day, the youngest rating on board donned the Admiral's hat. All his orders had to be obeyed. The Christmas festivities continued with the 'Lost Souls Choral Society' touring the ship with a portable organ powered by a vacuum cleaner, and ended with a giant conga dance into the royal apartments, the Prince bringing up the rear. He took part with gusto in other eccentric activities: a 300-yard horse race on the Falklands; a quaint 'pillow dance' on Tristan da Cunha; and a day out hunting crocodiles in The Gambia. During the tour, *Britannia* sailed 31,430 miles, crossed the equator three times and proved beyond doubt her worth to the Queen and Commonwealth.

But in these journeys, Prince Philip was essentially visiting the outer reaches of the Commonwealth. When it comes to contacts with Australia and Canada, it is the Queen herself who goes. As one royal courtier put it, 'In a changing world, the Queen feels she is the last link between our island and the two former great dominions.'

When the Queen cruised down the great St Lawrence Seaway in 1959 for the grand opening ceremony, *Britannia* was specially modified for the journey. A 20-ft (6-m) section of her main mast was hinged so that she would pass under the bridges, and an elm fender was put round her hull for protection. During this tour the Queen made her first TV appearance. The producer found her intensely nervous in front of the camera, but then Prince Philip stepped up and said, 'Remind her of the weeping and the gnashing of teeth.' His cryptic message did the trick, and the broadcast went ahead successfully.

More importantly, the Queen was nursing a secret – she was expecting her third child, Prince Andrew. When she welcomed her guests – Canada's Prime Minister John Diefenbaker, the American President Dwight Eisenhower and his wife Mamie – she took the latter aside into her sitting room and gave her the good news. Later as she stood on deck with them, an American senator standing among the cheering crowd shouted, 'We have all fallen in love with the Queen, Ike.'

It was fitting that Prince Andrew should spend some time at school in Canada just as Prince Charles had in Australia. The affinity of the royal family with these two countries is matched by the frequency with which *Britannia* is seen in the harbours of Sydney and Melbourne.

Indeed Australia and New Zealand were chosen as the centre-pieces of the Commonwealth Tour of 1953/4 that was to be the fanfare for the new Elizabethan age. It was an exhausting programme that encompassed 10,000 miles by plane, 900 miles by car, 2500 by rail and the rest on the cruise liner *Gothic*, especially converted for the Queen's use. The Queen and Prince Philip went alone, and after five months' absence from their two children, they decided to use *Britannia* on her maiden voyage for a family reunion in Tobruk.

Family reunion

And so it was that, in April 1954, accompanied by two nannies and a governess, Prince Charles and Princess Anne journeyed down to Portsmouth to board *Britannia*. Charles said goodbye to his pet white rabbit 'Harvey', leaving it in the tender care of the Buckingham Palace gardener.

At Portsmouth, they were met by the Lord Mayor before marching smartly up the gangway of the royal yacht. As they came aboard, the ship's company formed a guard of honour, and Charles, then a rather solemn five year old, walked slowly along the line of sailors carrying out his first royal inspection. His sister somewhat spoiled the effect by saying 'how do you do' and sticking out her hand as she passed by each man.

The ship was equipped with a sandpit, a slide, and two 'pedal-car' models of the yacht. Four ratings, the best swimmers on the ship, were deputed to mind the royal pair. A farewell wave to the Queen Mother and Princess Margaret on the quayside, and the royal youngsters were off on their voyage of discovery.

Princess Anne brought her teddy-bear, dolls and doll's house because she thought the sea air would do them good, and Charles continued his dancing and school lessons for an hour each morning before going off to explore. The crew made them buckets and brushes marked with their names, gave them mops and miniature lengths of hose. The young royals joyfully rolled up their dungarees, took off their shoes and helped swab the deck. Even today the decks gleam like bleached bones and guests who travel on board are discreetly asked not to use suntan oil as it stains the wood.

The Prince and Princess also visited the gleaming engine room and were entertained at night by Walt Disney films.

Right: Princess Margaret and the Queen Mother wave goodbye to Prince Charles and Princess Anne from the quayside at Portsmouth, as Britannia embarks on her maiden voyage in 1954.

Above: The royal children, their nannies standing behind them, take in the exciting scene as they leave Portsmouth for a reunion with their parents in Tobruk. During the Queen's 1954 Commonwealth tour Prince Charles learned to read.

When they reached Malta, they joined Uncle Dickie – Lord Mountbatten – and spent a week playing in the rock pools of Gozo, soaking up the sun. When they arrived in Tobruk, the Queen and Prince Philip, with King Idris of Libya, watched the royal yacht bringing their two children for a joyful and tearful reunion. As the Queen was piped aboard her floating palace for the first time, Charles had to be stopped from joining the receiving line of officers waiting proudly for Her Majesty.

Once on board, she reviewed the Mediterranean Fleet led by Lord Mountbatten who, with his customary verve and panache, sailed the Navy ships so close to the royal yacht that the delighted Queen was splashed by the spray. He later joined the royal party in spectacular style, swinging in a jack-stay from his flagship HMS *Glasgow*. Although a maiden voyage, there was an end-of-term atmosphere on board. Legend has it that the excited Queen tried out the radio to find out how one of her horses had fared.

At Gibraltar Prince Charles cautiously fed a group of Barbary apes while his sister joyfully ran through them scattering peanuts everywhere. As they sailed away from the island, the Royal Marine band serenaded the royals with a rendition of 'Greensleeves', and so excited by the whole adventure was Princess Anne that she climbed a ladder on the ship and refused to come down until her father tugged her down.

The flags and the fleet were out in force as the royal yacht steamed into home waters. Prime Minister Winston Churchill thought it only proper that he should join his beloved Queen when *Britannia* sailed into the Pool of London. He and other dignitaries travelled down to Southampton to join the ship off the Needles. Sir Hugh Casson, designer of the interior, was among the party, and in his diary for 1980 he paints a vivid and memorable picture of the homecoming:

'The Prime Minister in the admiral's barge, cigar stuck in smile, waving his little taxi-driver hat to the escorting yachts . . . *Britannia* looking impossibly tall and heraldic . . . the Fleet reviewed . . . the excited, sleepless night aboard . . . the end-of-term atmosphere as we entered the Thames estuary . . . two men in trilby hats boiling shrimps in a small boat off Gravesend . . . Tower Bridge and the fur-hatted Lord Mayor in an open boat with upraised oars . . . *Britannia*'s captain Commander Dalgleish (with a broken ankle) hopping agonizedly from one side of the bridge to the other as we moor up, determinedly without tugs ('The Navy doesn't use tugs') . . . the lunch party and family reunion . . . the boatloads disappearing in order of grandeur (Royals . . . entourage . . . personal staff . . . luggage . . . finally, after a cup of tea, the Admiral, now bowler-hatted, and me).'

The end-of-term jollity was somewhat taken advantage of by Churchill's valet who, during a feature film laid on for the Prime Minister, became rather drunk after enjoying *Britannia*'s liberal hospitality in the mess. For the first time in years Churchill had to put himself to bed – after first he and then his private secretary, Colville, rolled the inebriated servant into his bunk with 'many admonitory remarks'.

During the momentous voyage up the Thames, both Prince Charles and Princess Anne got in on the act, spending their time calling down to the Trinity House pilot Herbert Wynn. 'All the way up river the royal children were shouting down a voice pipe to me,' he recalls. 'They were telling me to "look at this and look at that" and Princess Anne said, "What a funny voice you've got."'

As usual *Britannia* shooed away the proffered tugs and slowly made her way up a difficult tide, 'as awkward as you can get,' said the pilot. 'The slightest mistake and we might easily have hit crowded vessels or piers.'

The Queen was home, and *Britannia*, her hold weighed down with presents, was immediately taken to the nation's heart. Over the years she has become a veritable treasure trove of diamonds, rubies, spears, swords and gold. After one visit to Canada the royal yacht groaned her way home with 400 items on board including a pair of snow shoes, a £5000 mink coat, a chunk of iron ore, a 5ft statue of a bucking bronco, a sackful of spears and polo sticks, a 15ft motor boat, a syrup jug and a painting of a power station. A mere five days in Australia resulted in 26 gifts including a bronze cauldron, a pair of ponies, a wooden chest and an umbrella. On that historic first Commonwealth voyage the Queen was given a brooch of very rare yellow diamonds in the form of a wattle, the national emblem of Australia – a deft transition from gift to regal symbol.

These tributes, although spectacular, pale by the side of the Alladin's Cave of gifts the *Britannia* brought home with her when the Queen went to fly the flag in the Arabian Gulf in 1979. If she had wished she could have turned the Union Jack into a star spangled banner of diamonds, sapphires and rubies. Her path as she made her way through Bahrain, Qatar and other Gulf States was strewn with gold. More than a million pounds' worth of treasures were taken back, labelled and displayed in the royal residences. Diamond-studded watches, huge natural pearls, a gold handbag and pinafore of gold chainmail were showered on the Queen. Even she, who has one of the biggest collections of jewellery in the world, was dazzled by the display. Prince Philip was not neglected, being given a gold sword with a mother of pearl inlaid handle and a scabbard encrusted with diamonds and rubies. Every time they returned from visits to Kuwait, Bahrain, Saudi Arabia and Qatar the strongroom of *Britannia* became more crowded. The Queen's return gifts were silver salvers with the royal yacht engraved on them and in some cases a book on Bedouin jewellery.

Apart from these riches that the Queen has brought home, *Britannia* herself is a treasure store of memories. An album of snapshots going back 31 years. Like the time millions of television viewers saw *Britannia*, her white superstructure and buff funnels glide away from Fiji into the deep Pacific night with islanders singing softly on the quayside and the Queen in evening dress and tiara waving a fond farewell. Or of Princess Diana standing on deck at midnight, camera snapping away as *Britannia*'s spotlight lit up the pale blues and greens of a giant iceberg in the mouth of St Johns harbour. Or the scent of a million rose petals scattered by native girls as the yacht entered Bangkok. Or of the Queen Mother, reassuring in her familiar blue chiffon dress, waving to the survivors of the Falklands War, cheering with tears in their eyes as they sailed by on board the *QE2* to an emotional homecoming at Southampton.

Yes, always the sound of cheering.

Of such memories legends are born . . . and *Britannia* is certainly legendary.

Opposite, top left: Princess Margaret shows the Queen her Caribbean hideaway, the island of Mustique, during a visit in 1977. To the left of the picture is the famous Basil's Bar, where Princess Margaret often goes to relax with her friends.

Opposite, top right: During a visit to Dubai in 1979, the Queen accepts a gift from Sheik Rashid, a solid gold camel (with palm trees) eighteen inches (46 cm) high. It is used as a table decoration for dinners on board Britannia.

Opposite, below: A group of expatriate Britons watches Britannia sail by the Samoan shoreline in 1977.

6

HONEYMOON HOTEL

'There are 276 men on board Britannia and every one is in love with Princess Diana'

ROYAL YACHT RATING
AFTER THE MEDITERRANEAN CRUISE

A honeymoon with 270-odd other men is hardly every bride's dream of the ideal way to start her married life. But then again royal brides are rather special, and the royal yacht *Britannia* no ordinary ship. As the Princess of Wales wiped the tears from her eyes and watched the hooting, honking armada fade gradually into the distance, nothing could have been more perfect than a sun-drenched saunter around the Mediterranean. For the first time in eight months of anxiety and heart searching, she was truly alone with her husband, away from the prying eyes and lenses of the world. The ship's company was under strict orders to keep away from the royal apartments at all costs. Royal servants were down to the bare minimum – an equerry, a private secretary, a valet, two detectives and a maid. *Britannia* was the perfect vehicle for a get-away-from-it-all honeymoon. 'It was good fun,' recalls Rear

Right: Welcome aboard. Princess Diana swaps her open-topped Triumph Stag for a berth on board Britannia. *This was the end of an exciting day, a day on which she and Prince Charles had driven through the flag-bedecked streets of Gibraltar.*

Previous page: With tears in her eyes and her husband by her side, the Princess of Wales watches the flotilla of hooting, honking boats bid her farewell from Gibraltar harbour.

Admiral Paul Greening. 'Our aim was to give them a bit of peace and quiet, and I think we succeeded. Anywhere they wanted to go we took them. We wanted to make sure they had as happy a honeymoon as possible.'

After all, royal yachts are used to romance. The autumn of 1677 saw the marriage of William of Orange to Mary, the daughter of James, Duke of York. They chose the second royal yacht *Mary*, a 166-ton vessel completed that year, for a cruise over to Holland. The royal couple, accompanied by King Charles II, the Duke of York, and other nobility, left Whitehall in barges for Erith where the yacht awaited them.

It was a summer cruise on *Britannia*'s predecessor, the *Victoria and Albert*, which was to prove the vehicle for the most momentous meeting in the history of the House of Windsor.

On the afternoon of July 22nd, 1939, the *Victoria and Albert* dropped anchor on the River Dart, and the King and Queen, together with the two princesses Elizabeth and Margaret, along with Lord Louis Mountbatten, marched up the steps to the Naval College in the pouring rain. While the two Princesses played croquet, they were introduced to Cadet Captain Prince Philip of Greece, Lord Mountbatten's nephew. That evening he came on board the yacht for dinner.

On the following afternoon, the *Victoria and Albert* steamed out of the harbour mouth, leaving behind a saluting flotilla of 109 small craft. However, the 110th continued to follow in the ship's wake, pitching and rolling crazily. The lone oarsman was the young Prince, and on deck, Princess Elizabeth, then thirteen, watched his unsteady progress through a pair of binoculars.

'That damn young fool,' cried the King, and it was only when the bellowed command of Uncle Dickie reached him that Philip finally returned to the College. The rest is history.

Although the royal couple could not use *Britannia* for their own honeymoon, they did manage to take her for a romantic holiday in the Mediterranean in 1956. The Queen flew out to join Prince Philip for this 'second honeymoon' after he had taken part in a series of Fleet exercises. They cruised lazily along the rocky coasts of Corsica and Sardinia, enjoying picnics in sheltered coves and roaming inland incognito. During one informal sight-seeing session, the Queen, dressed in slacks, blouse and headscarf, was met by a Corsican peasant woman who, in halting English, asked if she could be directed to 'the Queen of England's big ship' which she very much wanted to see. Kindly, the Queen pointed out the way, but kept her identity a secret.

A time to remember

During her Mediterranean cruise with Diana and Charles, *Britannia* managed to keep herself so secret that the romantic Italian press dubbed her 'the ghost ship'. Like everything else on *Britannia* this 'vanishing act' could all be attributed to detailed planning. While Diana was saying 'I do' in St Paul's, the ship's company was busily putting the finishing touches to the yacht in Gibraltar Harbour, buffing up the brasses, bringing fresh vegetables on board from North Africa, and carrying the trunks of clothes to the royal apartments. 'And don't forget Charlie's windsurfer,' was the cry from the quayside. They didn't.

After spending their first night together in the splendour of Broadlands, the late Lord Mountbatten's home, the newlyweds flew to Gibraltar, Prince Charles at the controls of an Andover of the Queen's flight. Possibly because of the row there had been over the cruise beginning from this disputed territory – the Spanish royal couple did not attend the wedding – Charles and Diana got a bigger send-off than expected. Everyone in Gibraltar turned out to wish them 'bon voyage', and when the Prince and Princess made their way through the cheering, singing throng in an open-topped Triumph Stag, they were left in no doubt as to what everyone thought of the match. Confetti flew everywhere, and flags that had been kept in mothballs since the 1953 Coronation were unfurled. Everyone went carnival crazy. As they walked slowly up the gangway of the royal yacht a tremendous roar of appreciation went up from the crowd, and it wasn't long before they were demanding an encore, shouting, 'We want the royal couple.' They were rewarded when the smiling pair came out on the sun deck to wave for the departure.

A twenty-one gun salute roared out from the naval shore base at HMS *Rooke*, and the personal standard of Prince Charles was broken at the yacht's

main mast. Before leaving, the royal couple entertained the Governor of the Colony and local dignitaries to drinks. One visitor, Lady Hassan, wife of the colony's chief Minister, revealed, 'It was wonderful. . . . They stood hand in hand while we chatted and kept looking into each other's eyes. It was beautiful to see two young people so devoted. The Princess was very moved by the welcome. She kept peering out of the porthole and tears welled in her eyes. She was overwhelmed by it all.'

The guests said their fond farewells, and at 6.45p.m. the yacht weighed anchor and put out to sea, followed by a riotous assembly of small boats. Church bells rang, crowds lined the shoreline, the band of the First Staffords on the quay played 'Sailing'. Diana settled in the crook of her husband's arm and in between waving, wiped the tears from her eyes. Slowly the yacht slid out into Algeciras Bay, the sun sinking in the distance. 'Destination unknown' was the signal from the bridge.

For the next two weeks they wandered wherever they wished, heading gently eastwards to the Suez Canal and a meeting with President Sadat of Egypt. While Diana lay lazily on deck slowly baking golden brown, a battalion of photographers and reporters was getting hotter and hotter under its collective collar as they frenziedly scoured the seas and shores for a sighting of the elusive couple. Not a stone, rockpool, lagoon or marina was left unturned in the elaborate cat and mouse game. The mouse in this case was Prince Charles's assistant private secretary Francis Cornish, who had planned a series of routes before leaving Buckingham Palace.

Above: Destination unknown. Britannia sails into the sunset for lazy days wandering in the Mediterranean. The route was a closely guarded secret.

Right: The Princess of Wales in her trendy tropical rig goes on a voyage of exploration round her temporary home.

As the yacht sailed on, hugging the coast of Algeria, across to the toe of Italy and down through the Greek islands to the Red Sea, Francis would join the yacht from time to time, brought on board by a royal barge. It was his job to observe all the formalities and courtesies on behalf of Prince Charles and ensure there were no hiccups on the way. Many people forget that *Britannia* is a Royal Navy ship and so cannot simply gatecrash another country's coastal waters.

Every morning Rear Admiral Greening would chat to the couple about the route, and they both decided where they should go. 'There was no set plan,' he says, 'just a number of options, bearing in mind we had to head east all the time. I would say to them "Look, we can picnic here, or stay at sea or visit this island here. The final decision was always up to them."'

As for the newshounds champing at the bit . . . 'The trouble with them was that they worked against themselves because they were in competition. If they had worked as a team we might have had trouble. But at the very worst we could always have stayed at sea.'

Everyone co-operated to give the honeymooners the time of their lives. The Greek Navy helped by warning off a party of cameramen who hired a helicopter to spot the yacht. They were told they would be shot down if they tried. A British reporter was tipped off to 'fly to Morocco . . . they might be here . . .' When he told his newsdesk that the only plane available was a private air-conditioned jet costing £1800 for the forty-five minute journey, the order came back, 'Hire it.' After a pleasant flight relaxing in fur-lined seats and sipping champagne, the reporter landed in Morocco, but failed to find the royal couple, and ended up clinging to the side of a jolting, battered bus in search of a room for the night.

While newsmen were rushing round with increasing frenzy, life on board the yacht could not have been more relaxed. Prince Charles decided to forego his usual 8a.m. breakfast call, sleeping in late and dining off a breakfast tray brought by a steward. (The romantic royal had had the foresight to bring his own double bed – *Britannia* lacks this one honeymoon essential.) After breakfast Diana would exercise to a 'workout' tape or listen to music on her portable stereo she took on board – Dire Straits, Elton John and Neil Diamond were some of the favourites. The Princess used the Queen's bedroom as a dressing-room, and the couple spent much of their time in the glassed-in sitting room on the royal deck, or simply soaking up the sun on the veranda.

They would swim in the yacht's canvas pool, and often, the yacht would weigh anchor, the barges be lowered, and they would take the plunge at one end of the ship, with the crew swimming at the other. Charles taught his wife how to windsurf as they cruised among the Greek islands.

The Royal Marine band had little to do as the honeymoon couple ate in their sitting room rather than the vast dining room. Occasionally they would watch films like *Chariots of Fire* after dinner with the royal staff. Videotapes of the royal wedding had been dropped on board from a helicopter, and there were giggles galore over Diana's gaffe when she got Charles' names in the wrong order during the ceremony at St Paul's.

One day the even tempo of the cruise was disturbed when the radio room on *Britannia's* escort ship, the frigate *Amazon*, picked up an SOS message from a woman in a motor cruiser. As it was only five miles from the Sardinian coast the more cynical members of the royal yacht thought it was a newshound working on the principle that if she couldn't get to the honeymooning couple, they could be persuaded to come to her. However, it turned out that the boat's owner was a British woman who had bought the cruiser at the Boat Show simply because 'she liked the interior fittings,' and she and her Finnish mate had got lost. *Britannia* soon set them on their way.

Above: *A flotilla of boats greets*
Britannia *as she sails into Port Said.*

Right: *Relaxed and tanned, the Prince
and Princess of Wales entertain
President Anwar and Jihan Sadat to
dinner on board* Britannia. *The two
couples achieved a friendly rapport which
made the news of Sadat's assassination
several weeks later all the harder to bear.*

While Charles lay sunning himself Diana would explore the yacht, visiting the kitchens to choose the menu – ice cream was a royal favourite – or chatting to the officers and ratings. Very quickly the traditional reserve of the Senior Service vanished. One awestruck rating said, 'Quite frankly we get a bit blasé about seeing the royal family, but with the Princess it's quite the opposite, she is sensational.'

Another commented, 'All the sailors on board bubbled over with stories like, "She spoke to me today," or "She cracked a joke with me."'

She won over the hearts of the ship's company – if any still needed winning – when she joined in a singsong in the sailors' mess. One rating describes how, 'without warning she appeared at the door of the mess where a group of sailors were having a drink and singing songs around the piano. Of course when everyone saw her the music stopped and the place went quiet. You could have heard a pin drop.'

But Diana would have none of it. She sat down at the piano and started playing the song they had been singing, 'What Shall We Do With a Drunken Sailor?' She was offered and surprisingly accepted a can of beer. 'We were all tickled pink,' says one. Then it was their turn to respond. The pianist slipped onto the seat and started playing the old Paul Anka hit song, 'Diana'. When it got to the line, 'Stay By Me Diana' everyone joined in lustily. 'I'm sorry I've got to go,' said the smiling Princess as she was gently led upstairs by several petty officers. As she left, all the ratings gave her a rousing cheer.

She still remembered the incident when she again visited the mess during her Canadian tour two years later. Indeed, such is her affection for the yacht that during that visit she went to the NAAFI shop and bought a pale blue T-shirt with the *Britannia* logo on the front for baby Prince William. When one of the ratings remarked that it was a bit big for the young Prince she replied, 'No, he's huge. If he keeps growing at the rate he's doing now, he'll be bigger than both of us.'

Everyone on board was struck by the way she easily related to them all – from the Admiral to the stokers. 'She appreciates the job we do,' said one rating. Indeed, during her Canada tour, she and Prince Charles took the trouble to pose for pictures with twelve members of the ship's company who had fought in the Falklands War. It was the first time for many years that this tribute had been paid. 'All the men were very pleased. It made them the envy of all their friends,' commented Commander Simon Sloot.

Diana's high spirits and playful sense of fun helped to make the honeymoon cruise an enjoyable experience for everyone. During one afternoon, the royal couple came aboard after they had been swimming and sunbathing on one of the Greek islands. They were in a playful mood. Diana darted ahead of Charles up the gangway, realizing that he had to proceed at a slightly more dignified pace and take the salute from the officers who were on duty at the head of the gangway.

As he saluted the officers the playful Princess dashed out with a bucket of water and tipped it over his head. As one sailor said, 'Charles looked a sight, dripping on deck, while his bride laughed at his discomfort. He leapt in surprise as the water hit him. Then, realizing what had happened, chased after the Princess. It was a sight to behold.'

Of course no royal cruise would be complete without a feast of beach barbecues, and Diana's honeymoon was no exception. Coves and beaches were chosen which were virtually inaccessible by land. Even so, before the royal couple disembarked on the royal barge, the two detectives, Superintendent John MacLean and Inspector Graham Smith, would go ashore first to scout round.

One moonlit night they enjoyed a barbecue in a bay on the coast of Ithaca.

Above: Prince Charles in his red swimming trunks surveys the scene at Port Said.

It was organized by the yacht's officers, who did all the cooking – even for th Buckingham Palace chef. After they had eaten, a Royal Marine accordioni came ashore, song sheets were handed out, and the night air rang to the soun of Boy Scout songs and sea shanties, with a royal soprano ringing out abov the deep bass of the officers and staff.

One afternoon picnic turned into a riot of fun when Diana played practical joke on the Prince. As he relaxed in a beach chair in his trunks, th Princess crept up behind him with a handful of ice which she had grabbed fro the cooler. Grinning from ear to ear, she carefully placed it on his stomacl shouting, 'This will cool you down,' before running off down the beach wit Charles in hot pursuit.

The yacht sailed on, visiting the spectacular volcanic island of Santorin reputed to be the site of the lost city of Atlantis. From here they sailed eas cruising through the Dodecanese Islands, past Rhodes until they reached Po Said and dinner with Egypt's President Sadat and his English-born wife, Jihar It was their only official engagement, and the two couples achieved a rappo during their intimate dinner on board which made Sadat's assassination a fe weeks later all the harder to bear.

Before the meal, the Sadats presented the royal couple with their weddir gifts; a box for Prince Charles and jewellery for Diana. After dinner, th President decorated the Prince with one of Egypt's highest honours, the Ord of the Republic, First Class. At midnight, after the Sadats had made the farewells, the royal yacht weighed anchor and sailed down the 103 miles (16(km) of the Suez Canal to the Red Sea and the final leg of the voyage. The passed bunkers, wrecked tanks, burnt-out trucks, and accepted salutes an greetings from merchant and warships on the steam south. A launch delivere a bouquet of roses and lilies from five Egyptian couples who had married th day; Diana was delighted.

But all good things must come to an end. On the final day they swam in th warm Red Sea, Charles donning snorkel gear to look at the coral at clo quarters. A sharper lookout was kept when they heard that the sailors ha caught a shark on a fishing trip. (During a visit to Queensland, Australia, on Britannia angler caught a 169-lb (80-kg) grey shark from the deck. It was du despatched, but not before the captain cancelled his water skiing!)

Above: Britannia sails slowly through the Suez Canal, passing wreckage of the Arab-Israeli wars on the way.

Right: Princess Diana steps on to the red carpet laid on the desert sand outside Cairo. As Prince Philip once said: 'The man who invented the red carpet needed his head examining.'

In its own way the honeymoon finale was just as grand as its opening. For days the officers and men had been rehearsing a farewell concert. There were more than fourteen acts, from stand-up comics to bawdy singalongs. One beefy matelot, dressed as Lady Diana, had everyone in stitches, but the royal detectives and other members of the Household stole the show with their own version of the Rod Stewart song 'We Are Sailing'. It became 'We Are Loafing', and Diana's bikini-clad maid, Evelyn Bagley, held up a cue card for the new lyrics. Diana and Charles joined in the singsongs, the Princess playing the piano for one number.

The perfect end to a perfect honeymoon. When the royal couple flew back to Scotland to join the rest of the royal family at Balmoral, no one begrudged them their healthy tans or their splendid Mediterranean voyage.

Right: Honeymoon happiness. The royal yacht played a major part in enabling the royal couple to enjoy a trouble-free cruise in the sun. As Rear Admiral Greening says, 'We wanted to make sure that they had as happy a honeymoon as possible.'

Above: Jet-lagged, Captain Mark Phillips and Princess Anne board Britannia *at Bridgetown, Barbados, for a sunshine cruise, but unfortunately it rained for the first few days and they were both seasick.*

A Caribbean not-quite idyll

Unfortunately, this was not the case for either of the two previous royal honeymoon couples – Princess Anne and Captain Mark Phillips, and Princess Margaret and Lord Snowdon. Before they set foot on *Britannia*, they had MPs spluttering with rage at the cost of their planned cruises.

When the Navy Secretary announced that *Britannia* had just completed a refit costing £1.7 million, there were calls that Anne and Mark should contribute to the cruise. The Minister, Anthony Buck, told MPs that indeed the royal couple were making a payment, and wished them a pleasant honeymoon. The *Daily Mirror* was not amused. 'Who,' it asked, 'had been the nameless donkey who landed them with this absurdly expensive yacht trip when all that the newly-weds need is a love-nest?'

Similarly, when Princess Margaret was to set sail, Labour MP Emrys Hughes picked out the £4000-a-week wage bill for the ship's company as cause for complaint.

But on board *Britannia* itself, the ratings were more interested in trying on their new uniforms made especially for Princess Anne's honeymoon by seamstresses in Plymouth. There was much debate as to how the blushing royal bride would react when she saw a saucy sign in the petty officers' mess. The brightly lit sign flashed 'The Verge Inn', but the men decided to keep the name of their bar even though they expected the royals to visit. One petty officer said, 'We are sure it won't cause the Princess any embarrassment. People are very broadminded these days.'

Britannia sailed from Portsmouth bound for the West Indies several weeks before the couple were married in Westminster Abbey on a chilly November day. On their wedding day they drove in an open carriage to the Royal Chelsea hospital before spending the night at Thatched Lodge Cottage in Richmond Park. For Captain Phillips it was the end of a nerve-racking day.

The following afternoon they boarded a Boeing 707, Zulu Foxtrot, and took their two first-class seats to fly to Barbados and meet up with their honeymoon yacht. As they boarded the yacht at Bridgetown, Barbados, onlookers noticed that Anne and Mark looked rather tired and pale after their eight-hour flight. But they managed a smile and a wave to the watching crowd as they said their farewells to the reception party led by Sir Winston and Lady Scott, the island's Governor-General who had travelled with them on the British Airways flight. As they stood on the floodlit deck, a white-helmeted police band pealed out calypso rhythms and the *Love Story* film theme.

Britannia is a popular ship around these parts. Islanders remember with gratitude when the royal yacht took the time to deliver four tons of much needed text books to local schools. The books were from Welsh colleges which had no further use for them and were going to burn them until the *Britannia* crew stepped in and offered to take them to the West Indies.

However, the first few honeymoon days were hardly a textbook example of sunny Caribbean weather. Rain, thunder and lightning greeted the royal couple when they awoke on their first morning afloat. Captain Philips said in an interview with Angela Rippon, 'For the first four days we were both seasick. After the wedding I was pole-axed, and whenever I get really tired, even now, I get shivery and a bit feverish. And that's exactly what happened. It wasn't a very good start.'

There was another storm, this time verbal, when an angry skipper accused the yacht of ignoring an SOS signal when the 110-ft (33.5-m) *Nation* hit a reef near Canouan. He claimed that rescue vessels could have done with her seaborne floodlights and sophisticated radar.

The plan on board *Britannia* was to cruise slowly round the islands, including Mustique, then sail through the Panama Canal and on to the chain

'For the first four days we were both seasick.'

CAPTAIN MARK PHILLIPS

of palm-fringed coral islands, the Galapagos. While *Britannia* steamed on to New Zealand to join the Queen for the Commonwealth Games, the plan was that the royal couple would board an aircraft of the Queen's flight for a twelve-day official tour of Ecuador and several West Indian nations, including Jamaica and Antigua.

In order to keep the Fleet Street flotilla at bay, the royal yacht captain Rear Admiral Richard Trowbridge devised the plan of dropping off the royal couple at a secluded island and then sailing away for the day in the opposite direction using *Britannia* as a decoy for the press boats. As evening fell they would return to pick up the royal couple, who had spent their day sunbathing on the beach, before steaming on through the night. They visited Mustique, the island where Princess Margaret has a home, and picnicked on the uninhabited Tobago Keys.

For the last leg of the honeymoon the weather was kinder, with temperatures in the eighties, giving them the opportunity to play deck quoits and sip Coke on the veranda deck. By 1 December they had sailed through the Panama Canal, stopping for three days at the fabulous Galapagos Islands to see the giant turtles and colourful tropical birds.

From there an Andover took them to Quito in Ecuador to begin their official engagements. Captain Phillips was determined not to let the side down. During their visits, they picnicked 11,000-ft (3350-m) up in the Andes on the slopes of Mount Catopaxi, where Anne and Mark wore bright ponchos bought in a street market in the dusty village of Saquisily. While they bargained, an ecstatic announcer shouted on the loudspeaker the information that 'The Queen of London and her husband Prince Philip Marks' were honouring their humble shopping centre.

While Princess Anne took the handshakes, salutes and receiving lines in her stride, her husband came away feeling 'totally, totally shattered'. He records of this time: 'At my first lunch I sat next to two ladies who couldn't speak a word of English – the only language they had was Spanish which I didn't know at all. All we could do was draw little pictures and make sounds to each other, which meant we ended up having a giggly lunch as a result.'

When the couple finally landed at Heathrow to spend Christmas at Windsor Castle with the Queen, Captain Phillips was in need of a holiday to recover from his honeymoon.

Below: Britannia *lies at anchor off the tropical island of Mustique while the royal honeymooners Princess Margaret and Anthony Armstrong Jones, now Lord Snowdon, spend a lazy day on the beach.*

Photographer's paradise

The Caribbean had also been the setting for Princess Margaret's six-week honeymoon in 1960. Five years earlier she had fallen in love with the lively spirits and *laissez-faire* ways of the men and women on these sun-kissed paradise islands.

The couple were in sparkling form as they drove at a snail's pace from Buckingham Palace, down the Mall, along the Strand and through a maze of narrow streets down to the river Thames where a freshly painted *Britannia* was waiting to welcome them, seventy painters having worked round the clock in Portsmouth dockyard to get her into tiptop condition. In all twenty-four gallons of navy blue, thirty gallons of white, and six gallons of buff paint had been needed, and, the scaffolding around the yacht took forty-three men four days to erect. Ironically, it was the Queen's Rolls Royce which needed a touch-up! As the cheering crowds pushed in on the royal couple, the car was scratched and marked.

Shrieking car horns, chiming church bells and a symphony of ship's sirens greeted the couple as they boarded the royal yacht. Princess Margaret's standard was broken at the main mast, and in her sunshine-yellow going-away outfit secretly designed by Victor Stiebel, she smiled and waved happily at the jubilant crowd. Her husband, Antony Armstrong-Jones, looked less certain and, as might be expected, rather more nervous.

As *Britannia* passed under the raised archways of Tower Bridge and past their secret love-nest at 59 Rotherhithe Street, they both gave a special wave for

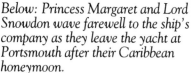

Below: Princess Margaret and Lord Snowdon wave farewell to the ship's company as they leave the yacht at Portsmouth after their Caribbean honeymoon.

'It was so wonderful for us both to lie on those deserted beaches without a soul in sight'

PRINCESS MARGARET

their friend and confidant, Bill Glenton, watching from the house window.

At Gravesend the promenade was crowded; on Southend Pier 10,000 waited to cheer *Britannia*. The town's mayor sent a message saying, 'Southend wishes every happiness to the bride and groom.'

They went on their way with the kind of send-off that only a royal yacht could provoke.

The Admiralty flashed a warning of rough weather and a floating mine ahead. However, *Britannia* made such smart progress that a pre-arranged rendezvous with a helicopter which planned to drop film and newspapers covering the royal wedding had to be scrapped.

As they made the 5000-mile journey south, they spent their days listening to Nat King Cole and Frank Sinatra records on the stereogram on the veranda deck. Before they arrived at Port of Spain in Trinidad to a rowdy, riotous reception, *Britannia* signalled ahead, 'Please respect the honeymoon.' Some chance. The air was as thick with the helicopters of French photographers as it was with flowers thrown at the couple. Steel bands greeted them in Trinidad, petals in Antigua and calypso singers on Dominica. They walked arm-in-arm along white beaches, took endless photographs, swam and picnicked on secluded beaches, like those on Robinson Crusoe Island, close to the famous underwater garden of Buccoo Reef. Next to the Golden Grove lagoon, *Britannia* anchored. For a time the couple used the beach cottage of a local planter, Mr Frank Latour, returning to the royal yacht at night. 'It was so very wonderful for us both,' said Margaret, 'just to lie on those deserted beaches without a soul in sight. Neither of us ever wanted to be rescued in the evening, and we would have gladly lived in a little grass hut.'

One day they visited the unknown island of Mustique – French for 'mosquito' – owned by Margaret's friend Colin Tennant. The flamboyant socialite bought the eight-square mile island in 1959 from two Irish spinsters for £45,000. Water had to be brought in from the nearby island of Bequia; there were no phones or roads, but the palm-fringed beaches and clear, warm waters made it a picture-postcard paradise. Colin Tennant had asked the Princess if she would like something wrapped in a box from Asprey's or a plot of land on Mustique as a wedding present. Margaret chose the land. When they all met up on the island the Princess was shown around by Colin and his wife. Eventually she picked a site overlooking Gelliceaux Bay in the south of the island, where was built a charming, cream-coloured plantation-style house called Les Jolies Eaux. To mark the event, the largest bay around the island was named after the royal yacht. Indeed the island has a regal flavour: the main street is called Royal Avenue, and Lord Lichfield has a home next door to Princess Margaret's.

In her drawing room, Margaret has a large portrait of the Queen. 'It's so that people from abroad can see it's an English house', she tells visitors.

Since Margaret adopted Mustique as her holiday hide-away, Mick Jagger, Raquel Welch and even Bob Dylan have all enjoyed the peace and seclusion of an island where goats and chickens roam free and where the odd monkey is kept as a pet. On that first visit the royal couple used the royal barge as a runabout around the island's bays, eating on *Britannia* at night.

The couple's welcome home from their honeymoon on 18 June was just as clamorous an affair as their departure. The ship's company lined the deck, and Princess Margaret – in a shocking-pink outfit – and a sun-tanned Tony Armstrong-Jones waved to the crowds on the shore and the myriad small craft bobbing about *Britannia*. As they drove off to their Kensington Palace home, sailors carried Margaret's three trunks down the gangway.

For the royal yacht, it was another role fulfilled; another performance over; another job well done . . .

7

INTO THE FUTURE

'The Queen's appearances abroad do more in a day to gain goodwill for Britain than all the politicians and diplomats lumped together could achieve in years.'

FORMER PRIME MINISTER
LORD HOME

A steel periscope pops its unblinking eye above the iron-grey waves of the Atlantic. Suddenly a dive bomber screams down from 30,000 feet, bombs ready to be released. In both their sights is the royal-blue hull of *Britannia*. The hunters and the hunted. It is the royal yacht performing yet another role in her repertoire, that of flagship for the NATO Fleet during exercises.

As it happened the imaginary bombs went wide and the royal yacht showed a clean pair of propellors to two chasing French submarines, the *Dauphin* and *Galetea*. Since 1968, when the Queen first gave the go-ahead to use her royal yacht in NATO exercises, she has taken part in twenty-two military excursions. Her sophisticated radar and satellite systems make her an ideal command centre or merchant ship.

Previous page: Flying the flag . . . as the Queen and Prince Philip leave Britannia *on the royal barge for a day of engagements in Stockholm, a group of Swedish businessmen was brought out to the yacht for a conference. Their discussions yielded contracts which have earned millions of pounds for Britain.*

Below: Workmen repaint Britannia *in preparation for Princess Margaret's honeymoon cruise. The expense of running the royal yacht has always prompted criticism, and on this occasion there were questions in the House of Commons from angry MPs.*

It was to armour the yacht against the constant broadsides of MPs over her running costs that the Queen allowed *Britannia* to be used in this way. From the moment her hull was laid down in 1952 the yacht has been under continual sniper fire, being dubbed 'a costly toy' and 'Philip's Folly' by pundits and parliamentarians alike. Every year since, she has faced similar cries of 'pension her off', 'put her into mothballs' or simply 'scrap her' from Labour, Liberal and even the occasional Tory MP.

In 1984 the royal yacht will cost the country £3 million to run – expenditure met by the Ministry of Defence. They will also have to pay out £6 million for a major refit – her third – to change her engines from using heavy fuel oil to using diesel, thus bringing her into line with the rest of the Fleet. Since she was built at a cost of £2,090,000 – even that figure came under attack because of the £200,000 extra paid in overtime to get her ready for her maiden voyage on time – in thirty years, *Britannia* has run up a bill of around £50 million at 1984 prices. Her running costs have risen from £29,000 in 1953–4 to £750,000 in 1970–1 to just over £8000 a day in 1983–4. At every refit questions are raised about the continuing cost. 'Nothing short of a national scandal,' stormed one Tory MP, and 'An expensive extravagance the nation can ill afford,' cried a Labour member when the latest refit was announced. On the yacht they treat the criticism with wry good humour. As one officer said, 'At £3 million a year we cost less than British Steel loses in forty-eight hours.' Pause. 'And that's better than it was. It used to be thirty-six hours.'

Top: Britannia *sails into New York on the final leg of the Queen's tour of America in 1976. While she was on land, the Queen gave permission for the yacht to be used as a business conference centre for the day. It is now planned to use* Britannia *as fully as possible in her export role.*

Above: Prince Philip greets a French Resistance veteran of the St-Nazaire raid of 1942. The survivors of this daring exploit are the only group ever to have used the yacht apart from the royal family.

However you look at it it's a lot of money, but the financial arguments for scrapping *Britannia* simply don't add up. Even if MPs succeeded in sinking her tomorrow the MoD would still have to shell out for the 276 officers and crew – a wage bill that accounts for nearly half the yacht's running costs. In addition the Foreign Office would have to beg, steal, rent or buy appropriate accommodation for the Queen when she visits abroad, and of course there would be the additional security headache. All of which adds up to a total that would make any savings look insignificant; indeed scrapping the yacht might even add to the Queen's costs without any corresponding benefits. And this ignores the positive prestige *Britannia*'s presence brings to Britain whilst abroad, and the sheer pleasure she gives the millions who have seen her over the years.

Despite this a large and flourishing School of 'Whynottery' appears to have set up a special course simply for *Britannia*. 'Why not put the Crown jewels into *Britannia* and send them both to American ports and Commonwealth countries? They would be a great dollar earner,' suggested Labour MP Emrys Hughes.

'Why not take old age pensioners on ten-day cruises or give infinite pleasure to retired pneumoconiotic miners and their wives,' suggested anti-monarchist MP Willie Hamilton. 'Why not use her for handicapped children, or why not a floating old folks home?' say others.

But in spite of all these suggestions only the Queen and members of her family have ever used the yacht, with just one exception. This was when the heroic survivors of the wartime raid on St-Nazaire made a commemorative voyage to France to mark the 40th anniversary of one of World War II's most daring episodes.

Prince Philip, who is patron of the St-Nazaire Society, gave permission for the 145 survivors to make this emotional journey back in time to what has often been called the greatest raid of all, when 630 sailors and commandos successfully blocked the strategic port of St-Nazaire, used as a submarine base by the Germans, by sailing directly in and scuttling an old American destroyer in the mouth. Five VCs were awarded, but in the hand-to-hand fighting 359 men were either killed or captured.

Among those on board for the commemoration was Captain Robert Ryder VC, who led the raid as a young naval lieutenant. 'It was a great honour for us to be allowed to use *Britannia*,' he says. Many survivors slept on the yacht's deck, and on the journey across the Channel they were serenaded by the Royal Marine band and a lone piper. It was a time of jokes and nostalgia as the survivors of Operation Chariot surveyed the concrete remains of the U-boat shelters. This sentimental occasion was invested with due ceremony by the use of the royal yacht.

While the use of and cost of the royal yacht continues to raise blood pressure in Britain, no one in Saudi Arabia raised an eyebrow when King Fahd decided to lavish £100 million on a new yacht. Ironically, the finishing touches – solid gold taps and handles, solid marble baths, bullet-proof glass and helicopter pads – were installed just a few miles down the coast at Southampton while *Britannia* was undergoing her controversial refit. This new yacht is called the *Abdul Aziz*, after a former Sultan of Turkey who came all the way to Britain in 1867 to be invested with the Order of the Garter by Queen Victoria. The place the Queen chose for the ceremony was the deck of the royal yacht, the *Victoria and Albert*.

The *Abdul Aziz* is one of the new wave of 'super yachts' being built around Europe. Since the war only a handful of large yachts have been constructed; besides *Britannia*, two river-class frigates were converted to yachts. The frigate *Annan* became the steam yacht *Moineau* in 1952, and the HMCS *Stormont* was converted to the yacht *Christina* for the ship-owner Aristotle Onassis in 1954.

Another flamboyant wheeler-dealer, arms magnate Adnan Khashoggi, is currently building a successor to his yacht *Nabila* in an Italian shipyard. It is only 400ft (122m) long – 12ft (3.6m) shorter than *Britannia*. The reason? He doesn't want it to outshine the Queen.

In recent years there has been a sea change in the way *Britannia* is used – a change that will please her critics, and a use that the ship's captain whole-heartedly approves of. On twelve different occasions now, *Britannia* has been used as a high-powered floating conference centre. Millions of dollars have been earned for Britain during these exercises, and in future royal tours will be linked to top-level conferences on board the yacht, so that as the Queen and Prince Philip fly the flag on land, *Britannia* herself spends a day at sea wooing bankers and industrialists who may invest in Britain or use British services. 'I can see nothing but good coming from this. It is a very useful and sensible use of the yacht,' says Rear Admiral Greening.

These 'Sea Days', as the navy calls them, started in a small way in 1963 when Prince Philip presided over a round-table talk on industrial and commercial relations with sixty employers and trade unionists in Australia. On a later occasion, after a day-long conference on *Britannia* during the Queen's three-week American tour in 1976, an American businessman

Above: Prince Philip escorts King Kahlid of Saudi Arabia on board for a banquet in 1979. The diplomatic use of the yacht is often underrated. An evening on board leaves a lasting impression in the minds of foreign dignitaries, an impression which is often reflected in future export orders.

Right: Best of British. The Queen and Prince Philip wave to Concorde *as she flies past* Britannia *on her way to New York.*

*'People seem to think that
we sit up a creek all year and
ooze out for Cowes week.'*

ROYAL YACHT OFFICER

declared enthusiastically, 'If you can do something like this you can't be such a bad country.'

A year earlier the royal yacht breezed into Vera Cruz and set a fair trade wind for a meeting between top Mexican and British industrialists to promote British trade.

But the cruise that the British Invisible Exports Council still waxes lyrical over was in 1981 when *Britannia* played host to Italian businessmen for the day. As they cruised round the Bay of Naples British bankers faced them in commercial combat. From that meeting 500 million US dollars' worth of business was generated, including 100 million US dollars for an Italian hydro-electric project in Colombia. The Council's director general William Clarke says, 'We carefully checked the business coming from that cruise and 500 million US dollars can be directly attributed to face-to-face contacts on *Britannia*. It is the ideal forum for the kind of business that depends on personal contact. The charisma of the royal yacht attracts high-calibre decision makers who wouldn't normally come to this kind of conference if it were held in a top hotel.'

As Rear Admiral Greening says, 'It's one thing to turn down a five-star hotel, quite another to refuse an invitation to come on board *Britannia*. No one ever does.' In 1983 normally reticent Swedish businessmen were coaxed into talking shop with twenty City of London bankers. The seventy names – all from the First Division of Swedish commerce – were offered the incentives of a day on *Britannia*. Again not one turned it down, and invisible export experts are delighted with the products from this Sea Day. 'The result is expected to be in hundreds of millions of pounds sterling', says William Clarke, the Council's director-general. Business so far includes a £32-million equity issue for a Swedish construction company by a London bank, financial cooperation in a Bombay port development bid, and an Indonesian hydro project. 'A significant proportion originated from contacts made on board the royal yacht', says Mr Clarke.

It's easy to understand that the Queen's floating palace is a more seductive atmosphere in which to wheel and deal than the traditional smoke-filled boardroom. To ensure that British bankers get the fairest trade wind possible to conduct their negotiations, *Britannia*'s officers organize the whole day with meticulous care. First comes the soft sell – a guided tour round the royal apartments and to that splendid engine room. Suitably impressed by Britain at her best, the hand-picked captains of industry are treated to a three-hour seminar while the yacht cruises carefully out to sea. Lunch is served in the dignified setting of the Queen's dining room while in the afternoon this captive audience, not bothered by phone calls or secretaries, talk hard-headed business. Contracts are not signed, sealed or delivered on *Britannia*, deals at this rarified level take months, even years to surface. When they do *Britannia* can take the (export) credit for providing a hothouse atmosphere where these hand-picked seedlings of trade can grow into money trees yielding dollars and kroners for Britain.

Sophisticated City export conferences are one thing, sample and fashion shows quite another. The Queen has no intention of devaluing *Britannia*'s hard-won currency in this way. As one courtier said: 'You have to keep the *gravitas* of the royal yacht, and bear in mind the serious fact that she is the Queen's residence at sea.'

As a travelling star of the world stage she has played many different roles, but first and foremost *Britannia* is a loyal servant of the Queen. In her own way the royal yacht is monarchy writ small, a magnificent mixture of the ancient and the absurd, of pomp and prestige, of seamanship and showmanship.

Long may this First Lady reign supreme over the seas.

1954   DIARY OF A ROYAL YACHT

1954

LIBYA	With Prince Charles and Princess Anne to Tobruk in April and May where the Queen and Prince Philip embarked for return to Britain following their Commonwealth tour.
CANADA	To Britain with Prince Philip after his three-week Canadian visit.

1955

WEST INDIES	Visited the West Indies with Princess Margaret.
MEDITERRANEAN	With Prince Philip, attended Combined Fleet Exercises in the Mediterranean.
NORWAY	Visited Oslo in June for the Queen's state visit to Norway.
WALES, ISLE OF MAN & SCOTLAND	In August the Queen, the Duke of Edinburgh, Prince Charles and Princess Anne made short visits to Wales, the Isle of Man and Scotland.
DENMARK	Prince Philip sailed to Copenhagen in October as guest of King Frederick.

1956

MEDITERRANEAN	With the Duke of Edinburgh attended the Fleet Exercises in the Mediterranean and afterwards, with the Queen, made private visits to Corsica and Sardinia.
SWEDEN	Visited Stockholm in June for the state visit to Sweden by the Queen and Duke of Edinburgh.
SCOTLAND	At Rothesay for the Duke of Edinburgh's visit to the Clyde Fortnight; later toured the Western Isles with the royal family.
KENYA, MAURITIUS, ZANZIBAR & TANGANYIKA	In September Princess Margaret embarked at Mombasa for a tour to Mauritius, Zanzibar and Tanganyika.

1956–57

WORLD TOUR	The Duke of Edinburgh joined at Mombasa where he embarked on his four-month world tour visiting the Seychelles Islands, Ceylon, Malaya, New Guinea, Australia (where he opened the Olympic Games in Melbourne), New Zealand, Antarctica, the Falkland Islands, South Georgia, Gough Island, Tristan da Cunha, St Helena, Ascension and The Gambia.

1957

PORTUGAL	From Setubal in Portugal to Lisbon for the state visit in February.
DENMARK	Visited Copenhagen in May where the Queen and Prince Philip made a state and private visit.
SCOTLAND	At Invergordon for the royal visit to the Home Fleet.
CHANNEL ISLANDS & ENGLAND	*Britannia* visited the Channel Islands in July with the Queen and afterwards at Cowes Week with the Duke of Edinburgh and Prince Charles.

1958

NETHERLANDS	Visited Amsterdam and Rotterdam in March during the Queen's state visit to the Netherlands.
NORTHERN IRELAND	In May took Queen Elizabeth the Queen Mother on a visit to Northern Ireland.
GREAT BRITAIN	In June visited ports on the east coast of England and in Scotland, with the Queen. Prince Philip visited the Scilly Isles, the Naval Colleges at Dartmouth and Plymouth, and Portsmouth. In August at Cowes, later a ten-day private cruise to the Western Isles.

BRITANNIA'S PRINCIPAL VOYAGES

1984

1959	PACIFIC ISLANDS, PANAMA & THE BAHAMAS	Following his tour of India and Pakistan, Prince Philip embarked at Rangoon for visits to Singapore, Sarawak, North Borneo, Hong Kong, the Solomon Islands, the Gilbert and Ellice Islands and Christmas Island.
	CANADA	In June the Queen and Prince Philip embarked at the mouth of the St Lawrence River for the official opening of the St Lawrence Seaway.
1960	CARIBBEAN ISLANDS	With the Princess Royal.
	WEST INDIES	With Princess Margaret and Mr Antony Armstrong-Jones.
	GREAT BRITAIN	To Cowes, Orkney and Shetland.
1961	GIBRALTER & TUNISIA	In April visited Gibralter and Tunisia with Queen Elizabeth the Queen Mother.
	ITALY	At Cagliari, Sardinia, the Queen and Prince Philip embarked for the state visit to Italy and the Vatican City, which included visits to Naples, Ancona and Venice.
	GREECE & TURKEY	With the Duke and Duchess of Gloucester.
	ENGLAND, N. IRELAND & SCOTLAND	With the Queen, sailed to Shotley, near Ipswich, and then to Portsmouth for Cowes Week, later a visit to Belfast and a cruise round the Scottish coast.
	GHANA, LIBERIA, SIERRA LEONE, THE GAMBIA & SENEGAL	In November the Queen and the Duke of Edinburgh embarked at Takoradi, Ghana, and then visited Monrovia, Freetown, Bathurst and Dakar.
1962	GIBRALTAR, CYPRUS & LIBYA	With the Princess Royal in February and March.
	ENGLAND	In April visited the Isles of Scilly with the Queen Mother. In July with the Queen and Prince Philip visits to Plymouth and Dartmouth; and in August Cowes Week.
1963	FIJI, NEW ZEALAND & AUSTRALIA	With the Queen and the Duke of Edinburgh.
	CHANNEL ISLANDS	With the Queen Mother.
	ISLE OF MAN & ENGLAND	In July visited the Isle of Man with the Queen Mother; and in August to Cowes.
1964	WEST INDIES	With the Queen Mother.
	SCOTLAND & ENGLAND	The east coast of Scotland with the Queen and Prince Philip.
	ICELAND	With Prince Philip, visited Reykjavik in June and July.
	CANADA	With the Princess Royal visited Newfoundland. With the Queen and Prince Philip visited Charlottetown to celebrate the centenary of the meeting of the Fathers of Confederation; then to Quebec.

1954 DIARY OF A ROYAL YACHT

	BAHAMAS & WEST INDIES	With Prince Philip.
1965	NETHERLANDS	Visited Amsterdam in May for British Week, with Princess Margaret and Lord Snowdon.
	FEDERAL REPUBLIC OF GERMANY	In May the Queen and Prince Philip embarked at Hamburg following a state visit.
	GREAT BRITAIN	Visited Cardiff, Kirkcudbright and Clydebank in June with the Queen and Prince Philip.
1966	WEST INDIES	With the Queen and Prince Philip.
	AUSTRALIA, FIJI & NEW ZEALAND	From March to May with the Queen Mother.
1967	CANADA	With the Queen and Prince Philip attended centennial celebrations and visited Expo '67 in Montreal.
1968	BRAZIL & CHILE	State visit by the Queen and Prince Philip.
1969	WALES	After the investiture of Prince Charles, toured Welsh ports.
	NORWAY	The royal family visited privately as guests of King Olav.
1970	FIJI, TONGA, NEW ZEALAND & AUSTRALIA	Bi-centenary celebrations of the voyage of Captain Cook.
	NORWAY & SCOTLAND	For NATO exercises (September).
1971	PANAMA CANAL ZONE & PACIFIC ISLANDS	A tour by Prince Philip, prior to his Australian tour in March.
	CANADA	The Queen, Prince Philip and Princess Anne toured British Columbia in May to mark the centennial.
	TURKEY	Visit by the Queen, Prince Philip and Princess Anne.
1972	SOUTH-EAST ASIA	The Queen, Prince Philip and Princess Anne visited among others Thailand, Singapore and Malaysia.
	CHANNEL ISLES	In May with Princess Anne.
		(From September 1972 to July 1973 the royal yacht underwent her first major
1973	WEST INDIES & GALAPAGOS ISLANDS	With Princess Anne and Captain Mark Phillips.
1974	NEW ZEALAND, FAR EAST & AUSTRALIA	The Queen and Prince Philip also visited the Norfolk Islands, the New Hebric the British Solomon Islands, Papua New Guinea and Indonesia.
1975	MEXICO	State visit by the Queen and Prince Philip.

BRITANNIA'S PRINCIPAL VOYAGES

1975 CENTRAL AMERICA — A tour, in March, by Prince Philip.

JAMAICA — A Commonwealth heads of Government meeting with the Queen and Prince Philip attending.

CHANNEL ISLANDS — A tour by the Queen Mother in May.

1976 FINLAND — In May the Queen and Prince Philip embarked for a state visit.

USA & CANADA — The Queen and Prince Philip joined *Britannia* in Bermuda for a visit to the USA. Then to Canada where the Queen opened the 1976 Olympic Games.

SCOTLAND — The Queen and Prince Philip visited the Western Islands of Scotland in August.

1977 SAMOA, TONGA, FIJI, NEW ZEALAND & AUSTRALIA — Jubilee Year, and in February, a tour by the Queen and Prince Philip to Australasia.

UNITED KINGDOM — Silver Jubilee tours of the east and west coasts of England and Wales, the West Country and N. Ireland; the Fleet review at Spithead on 28 June; attendance at Cowes Week during August, and a cruise to the Western Isles.

WEST INDIES — The Queen and Prince Philip paid visits in October and November to islands in the West Indies.

1978 FEDERAL REPUBLIC OF GERMANY — A state visit by the Queen and Prince Philip in May.

CHANNEL ISLANDS — With the Queen and Prince Philip to Jersey, Guernsey, Alderney and Sark.

WESTERN ISLES — After Cowes Week, the royals cruised to the Western Isles and paid an official visit to Orkney.

MEDITERRANEAN — NATO exercises during October.

1979 EASTERN ARABIA — With the Queen and Prince Philip.

DENMARK — A state visit in May.

GREAT BRITAIN — The Queen Mother visited the Clyde in June, and in July she was installed as Lord Warden of the Cinque Ports at Dover.

SCOTLAND — Cowes Week and the Western Isles.

(From September 1979–April 1980 *Britannia* entered dry dock for a refit.)

1980 ENGLAND — To the Pool of London for a Thanksgiving Service at St Paul's for the Queen Mother's eightieth birthday.

SCOTLAND — The Western Isles cruise included an official visit to Islay.

ITALY — State visits to Italy and the Vatican.

NORTH AFRICA — State visits to Tunisia, Algeria and Morocco.

1981 NORWAY — A state visit calling at Oslo and Stavanger.

SHETLANDS — With Prince Philip and King Olav of Norway, the Queen sailed to Sullom Voe where she inaugurated the oil terminal there.

1981 MEDITERRANEAN, INDIAN OCEAN & AUSTRALASIA
The Prince and Princess of Wales joined her at Gibraltar to spend two weeks of their honeymoon on board. They disembarked at Hurghada, Egypt and the royal yacht continued on to Melbourne. From Melbourne with the Queen and Prince Philip to New Zealand.

1982 FRANCE
During April to St-Nazaire with members of the St-Nazaire Society.

ENGLAND
In June, the Queen Mother welcomed home the survivors of HM ships *Coventry*, *Antelope* and *Ardent* from the Falklands.

AUSTRALIA & PACIFIC ISLANDS
After visiting the Commonwealth Games in Brisbane during October, the Queen and Prince Philip sailed to Papua New Guinea, the Solomon Islands, Nauru, Kiribati, Tuvalu and Fiji.

1983 MEXICO, USA & CANADA
During February and March the Queen and Prince Philip visited Jamaica, the Cayman Islands, Mexico, California and British Columbia.

SWEDEN
A state visit in May.

CANADA
In June the Prince and Princess of Wales included Nova Scotia, Prince Edward Island, Newfoundland and New Brunswick in their tour of Canada's eastern seaboard.

SCOTLAND
After Cowes Week in August, *Britannia* took the royal family on a tour of the Western Isles.

(During the winter of 1983–84 *Britannia* underwent a refit in which her boilers were converted to burn diesel fuel.)

1984 FRANCE
To mark the anniversary of the Normandy D-Day landings with the Queen and Prince Philip.

CHANNEL ISLANDS
With the Queen Mother.

CANADA
In September the Queen and Prince Philip paid a state visit to Canada, to mark the twenty-fifth anniversary of the opening of the St Lawrence Seaway.

ITALY
To Venice with the Queen Mother in October.

SUMMARY OF ROYAL DUTY – UP TO 1984

State visits	72
Visits with HM The Queen embarked but not state visits	154
Visits by other members of the Royal Family	190
Visits to Commonwealth countries by HM The Queen	72
Visits to Commonwealth countries by other members of the Royal Family	113
Visits in UK waters by HM The Queen	125
Visits in UK waters by other members of the Royal Family	69
Major exercises	10
Minor exercises	12
Sea Days (Business conventions)	12

SPECIFICATIONS

Built by John Brown and Co. Ltd., *Britannia* was laid down in June, 1952, launched at Clydebank on 16 April 1953, and commissioned in January 1954. She cost £2.1 million to build.

Her specifications include the following:

Length overall	412ft 3in (125.6m)
Beam	55ft (16.8m) maximum
Deep load displacement	4961 tons with 510 tons of fuel and 210 tons of fresh water
Gross tonnage	5769 tons
Mean draught	17ft (5.2m) at load displacement
Machinery	Two geared steam turbines developing 12,000-shaft horse power (8948 kilowatts) – two shafts
Speed	On trials – 22.5 knots at 4320 tons displacement Continuous seagoing – 21 knots
Endurance	At full fuel loads: 1776 miles at 20 knots 2452 miles at 18 knots 2822 miles at 14 knots

Construction

In constructing the royal yacht, aluminium alloy was used for the superstructure above the bridge deck and for the funnel; elsewhere steel was used because of its lower cost.

Britannia has Denny-Brown single fin stabilizers which can stabilize a roll of 20 degrees out to out, reducing it to 6 degrees at a ship speed of 17 knots.

Navigation

The navigational equipment carried on board enables *Britannia* to travel to most locations in the world. For pilotage waters, where very accurate navigation is necessary, an Admiralty Sperry Mk 5 (pattern 1005) Gyro Compass mounted deep in the structure transmits heading information to twelve repeaters throughout control positions in the yacht.

There are two echo-sounders, one shallow-water (0–100 fathoms/180m) Type 765 instrument, and one deep-water (0–4500 fathoms/8200m) Type 773 instrument, both manufactured by Kelvin Hughes.

An electromagnetic log registers speed through the water from a sensor head projecting through the hull. Distance travelled is measured by electronically comparing speed with a timebase in the instrument, and is displayed by mileometer on the bridge.

For offshore navigation, the primary method is by use of sextants and chronometers, in time-honoured fashion. As a backup for the celestial navigation method, the following electronic navigation systems are fitted:

   a. satellite transit navigation system (worldwide)
   b. medium-frequency direction-finder (1000 miles/1600km)
   c. Decca medium-frequency navigation system (0–250 miles/400km)
   d. Omega single-frequency VLF navigation system (worldwide).

HMY *Britannia*, in line with other ships of the Fleet, will soon be issued with the Howlett Packhard HP41C hand-held navigation computer to speed the reduction of celestial observations for offshore navigation.

For coastal navigation and pilotage in low visibility, there are two identical 3cm Type 1006 radar systems. Additional navigational instruments include optical range-fingers, Ziess and Barr & Stroud binoculars, a three-arm station pointer and normal drawing instruments.

Power

Following her latest refit (1983–4), the boilers no longer burn heavy oil, but diesel-fuel. Steam to drive the turbines is generated in two main boilers, each having a capacity of 75,000-lb/hr at a pressure of 300-lb/in and a temperature at the super heater outlet of 660°F (349°C). An auxiliary boiler is installed to meet harbour requirements. It has an evaporating capacity of 20,000-lb/hr at the same steam conditions as the main boilers, and can be used to augment the main steam supply.

The lighting and power are supplied by three 500-kW steam turbo-generators; one 270-kW diesel generator; and one 60-kW emergency diesel generator.

Boats

She carries with her:
One 41-ft (12.5-m) royal barge
Two 35-ft (10.7-m) medium-speed motor boats
One 32-ft (9.7-m) activity
Two 27-ft (8.2-m) jollyboats (sea boats)
Two 16-ft (4.9-m) fast motor dinghies
Two 14-ft (4.3-m) sailing dinghies

All power boats are diesel driven. *Britannia* also has 18 life rafts of a self-inflating type, and an inflatable raft to carry a Land Rover.

Radio

Britannia is well equipped with radios capable of transmission and with receptors ranging from medium to ultra high frequencies.

One set is provided with its own battery equipment for emergency use if all other power supplies, including the emergency generator should fail. A link is provided for ship-to-shore radio telephone communication, and on certain telephones speech can be 'scrambled' for privacy.

A satellite terminal is also fitted providing high-quality circuits for voice and telex transmission.

INDEX

BIBLIOGRAPHY

Argy, Josy and Riches, Wendy, *Britain's Royal Brides* (David & Charles, 1975)

Aronson, Theo, *Royal Family: Years of Transition* (John Murray, 1983)

Bennett, Sir John Wheeler-, *King George VI* (Macmillan, 1965 paperback)

Boothroyd, Basil, *Philip: an Informal Biography* (Longman, 1971)

Bradbury, Sue, Ed., *A Few Royal Occasions* (Michael Joseph, 1978)

Brown, Michele, *The Royal Yearbook: July 1977 – June 1978* (Pelham Books, 1978)

Campbell, Judith, *Anne: Portrait of a Princess* (Cassell, 1970)

Casson, Sir Hugh, *Diary* (new edn., Macmillan, 1982 paperback)

Cathcart, Helen, *Anne and the Princesses Royal* (new edn, Star Books, 1975)

Cathcart, Helen, *The Queen in Her Circle* (W.H. Allen, 1977)

Crabtree, Reginald, *Royal Yachts of Europe: From the Seventeenth to Twentieth Century* (David & Charles, 1975)

Crosland, Susan, *Tony Crosland* (Jonathan Cape, 1982)

Dixon, June, *Uffa Fox: a Personal Biography* (Angus & Robertson, 1978)

Drummond, Maldwin, *Saltwater Palaces* (Debrett's, 1979)

Duncan, Andrew, *The Reality of Monarchy* (Heinemann, 1970)

Fox, Uffa, *Sail and Power* (P. Davies, 1936)

Gavin, Commander C.M., *Royal Yachts* (privately published)

Grigsby, Joan Evelyn, *Annals of Our Royal Yachts, 1604–1953* (Adlard-Coles; George C. Harrap, 1953)

Hamilton, Willie, *My Queen and I* (new edn., Quartet Books, 1975)

Judd, Denis, *Prince Philip: a Biography* (new edn.,

New English Library, 1981 paperback)

Keay, Douglas, *Royal Pursuit: the Palace, the Press and the People* (Severn House, 1983)

Lane, Peter, *Prince Philip* (Robert Hale, 1980)

Lichfield, Patrick, *A Royal Album* (Elm Tree Books 1982)

Longford, Elizabeth, *Elizabeth R* (Weidenfeld & Nicolson, 1983)

McGowan, A.P., *Royal Yachts* (3rd edn., HMSO, 1977) (National Maritime Museum)

Morrow, Anne, *The Queen* (Granada, 1983)

Plumb, J.H., and Wheldon, Huw, *The Royal Heritage: the Reign of Elizabeth II* (BBC, 1981)

Queen's Regulations for the Royal Navy (revised edn. HMSO, 1967)

Rose, Kenneth, *King George V* (Weidenfeld & Nicolson, 1983)

Wakeford, Geoffrey, *His Royal Highness Charles, Prince of Wales* (Associated Newspapers, 1962)

Warwick, Christopher *Princess Margaret* (Weidenfeld & Nicolson, 1983)

PICTURE ACKNOWLEDGMENTS

Aspect: 77, 82; Associated Newspapers: 110; Beken of Cowes: 16t, 19r; Alastair Black: 50; British Movietone News Limited: 29; BBC Enterprises: 63b; BBC Hulton Picture Library: 8bl, 20b, 48t, 78, 108t, 108b; By permission of the Trustees of the Broadlands Archives: 21r; Camera Press: 98tr, 117t; Colour Library International: 8br; Express News & Features Service: 55bl; Jack Farley: 62; Reproduced by gracious permission of Her Majesty the Queen. Copyright reserved: 10, 13, 14t, 14b, 17tl, 17tr, 18b, 19l, 20t, 41l; HMY *Britannia* photographer Leading Airman Almond/MOD: 34t, 34b, 35t, 35b, 89t, 89b; HMY *Britannia* Archive/MOD: 28t, 28b, 38b, 44b, 47t, 57tr, 66, 73b, 75, 90, 93, 118b; Tim Graham: jacket, title page, 6, 8, 68, 73tr, 80b; Anwar Hussein: 46, 47b, 48b, 49, 71b, 79, 80t, 84, 85t, 85b, 88, 95tl, 95b, 98tl, 98b, 100, 102, 106t, 109, 111, 114, 118t; Illustrated London News/John Reader: 87; Keystone Press Agency: 52, 53, 56b, 57b, 63t, 71t, 76, 92, 96, 116; Patrick Lichfield/ Camera Press: 30, 39t, 39b, 42, 43r, 45, 73tl, 81; Bill Lucas: 61br; portrait of Prince William

originally appeared in the MENCAP Famous Faces Collection and is reproduced by kind permission of the Royal Society for Mentally Handicapped Children and Adults 41r; National Maritime Museum, Greenwich: 56t; Michael Parker © National Geographic Society: 38t, 94; Photographers International: 104; Popperfoto: 25, 43l, 57tl, 91; Press Association: 54t, 54b, 58; Rex Features: 58t, 70, 105t, 105m, 105b; St-Nazaire Society: 117b; John Shelley: 69, 95tr; Frank Spooner Pictures: 106b, 107; Syndication International: 61bl, 64; by courtesy of The Times: 24tl, 24r, 24bl, 40t, 40b, 44t; Topham Picture Library: 21l, 22, 23, 55t, 55br, 59t, 59b, 74, 97, 112; Topix, The Scotsman: 61t, 65.

Particular thanks to royal yacht photographer Leading Airman John Almond for his contribution to the book, and to Patrick Lichfield for making available unpublished photographs taken while a guest on board *Britannia* during the 1972 Silver Wedding Anniversary tour.

AUTHOR'S ACKNOWLEDGMENTS

Writing and researching material for this book has been a fascinating experience, which would not have been possible without the cooperation and assistance of the following people:
Sir Hugh Casson, Rear Admiral Paul Greening and Commander Simon Stone from the royal yacht, Michael Shea, John Haslam and Sarah Brennan from Buckingham Palace, and Frances Dimond, photographic curator at the Windsor Castle Archives.

At Orbis, special thanks must go to Sarah Coombe and Mia Stewart-Wilson for their picture research and assistance, while the help and advice from fellow royalty watchers, especially author Trevor Hall, has been invaluable. Grateful thanks also to my researcher Alistair McAlistair and to my wife Lynne for her patience.